The New Creation in Christ

Dedicated to the Founding Patrons of the
World Community for Christian Meditation,
Dom Bede Griffiths O.S.B.
and
Jane Blaffer Owen

The New Creation in Christ

Christian Meditation and Community

Bede Griffiths, OSB

Edited by
Robert Kiely and Laurence Freeman, OSB

Templegate Publishers
Springfield, Illinois

First published in 1992 by
Darton, Longman and Todd Ltd
1 Spencer Court
140-142 Wandsworth High St.
London SW18 4JJ

© 1992 Bede Griffiths OSB

ISBN 0-87243-209-2

First published in the United States of America in 1994 by
Templegate Publishers
302 East Adams Street
P.O. Box 5152
Springfield, Illinois 62705

Contents

Introduction by Laurence Freeman, OSB   **6**

Bede Griffiths Rest in Peace by Milo Coerper

1 The Monastic Ideal According to John Main   **14**

2 The Extension of the Monastic Ideal to the Laity   **25**

3 The Way of Meditation with a Mantra   **39**

4 Mantra Meditation in the Eastern Tradition   **58**

5 The Future of Contemplative Life in the Church   **74**

6 Questions and Responses   **87**

Writings of Bede Griffiths   **107**

Writings of John Main   **108**

The World Community for Christian Meditation   **109**

Introduction

Bede Griffiths met John Main in person only once. But, as this book shows, he came to know him very well through his books and through the community that grew out of his teaching. Of their single meeting in an American monastery in the summer of 1979 what I remember most vividly is their quick and shared sense of humour. Somewhat disconcerting their hosts, they would puncture the more solemn moments of discussion with free-spirited laughter and a sense of fun.

John Main often remarked that solemnity led to triviality while seriousness led to joy. Humour and simple jokes are not easy to convey in books; yet, for teachers whose first medium is the spoken word, the laughter of the spirit is a natural and essential channel for communicating the truth; or, we might say, for letting the truth out of the bag we tend to cram it into. At the John Main Seminar of 1991, at which Bede Griffiths spoke on the theme of 'Christian Meditation: the Evolving Tradition', there was this rare integration of seriousness and joy. Robert Kiely and I have tried in editing these talks to retain something of this quality of the oral tradition — the 'passing on' by word of mouth and by simple, total presence conveyed in the language of body, mind and spirit — in which we were then sharing so powerfully.

It was after John Main's death in 1982 that Father Bede first read him deeply. He wrote to me at about this time expressing his personal sympathy as well as his admiration for what John Main had attempted and begun in the community he founded in Montreal and which has now spread around the globe. It was then that I began to realize how much vision and common experience of hopes and disappointments these two quite different monastic prophets share.

John Main and Bede Griffiths, in the west and the east respectively, have each attempted to live a monastic life restored to its primitive essentials of contemplation and community. Both had known rejection and misunderstanding as well as some acclaim and recognition for their innovation. Father Bede understood how quickly people can leap on to the early failures of a new vision and use them to denounce the vision itself. He also knew that it was in small, risky communities rather than in comfortable institutions, and above all in faithfully returning to the call of the Spirit, that the vision is eventually realized.

Although their respective experiments in new kinds of monastic living were very different and answered the needs of different parts of the Catholic Church, Father Bede's deep and intuitive reading of Father John has brought the two movements together. This is the importance and the achievement of the teaching he gave at New Harmony, Indiana in August 1991 and which this book places on record for those who wish to share in that moment of the spirit at a distance of space and time.

When Father Bede wrote to me some years ago and said that he felt that 'in my experience John Main is the most important spiritual guide in the Church today', I replied by asking him what he meant by this. He was in no way diminishing the contribution of other contemporary teachers or wishing to create a competitive league table. What he meant was the uniqueness of the way John Main met certain critical needs of modern people in their search for a deeper experience of God.

Firstly, there was John Main's recovery of the tradition of the mantra within Christianity, in the teachings of the Desert Fathers and John Cassian in particular. This enabled the modern Christian to follow a method of contemplation with which he or she could feel theologically and culturally comfortable. And indeed, as Father Bede says in the following pages, this recovery of a way of

7

non-discursive meditation filled a tragic gap of several centuries in western Christian spiritual life.

Clearly what also delighted Father Bede about this was that Father John himself had first learned to meditate with an Indian teacher. It was this that opened his eyes to recognize that the 'formula' in Cassian's Tenth Conference is in practice the same as the 'mantra' of the east. Another great Benedictine scholar, Adalbert de Vogue, has said in his article 'From John Cassian to John Main' (*Monastic Studies,* no. 15) that just as Cassian bridges eastern and western Christianity so John Main is a bridge today between the Christian and non-Christian worlds.

Bede Griffiths himself, of course, is one of the great teachers of the marriage between east and west. More than John Main, he has made it his life's work to study and to be such a bridge. In this area they are clearly complementary and the differences between their teachings reflect gradations of emphasis and personal experience. For those who are made uneasy by Father Bede's yellow sannyasi robes or Sanskrit chant, Father John is a more familiar presenter of the teaching of non-duality. For those who find Father Main's single-minded focus on the mantra too demanding at first, Father Bede's cross-cultural and interdisciplinary thought gives a broader framework in which to begin meditating. Both are in no doubt, and do not hesitate to say, that the most important thing is to meditate.

Father Bede recognized in his early reading of John Main that one of his original contributions to the modern spiritual search was his special awareness of the connection between contemplation and community. By meditating in common, John Main's Benedictine communities and the global community of Christian meditation groups affirmed a truth which lies at the heart of his vision; that, out of the essential Christian experience of Christ within, the Church is born and grows. John Main was well aware that the birth of a community is also the beginning of the pain and growth and of the paschal cycles of development. If meditation creates community, community brings conflict. But this sword which Christ brings can also be used to cut away the layers of personal and collective egotism which obstruct the free passage of the Spirit.

Father Bede devotes some attention in the following pages to the individual's psychological experience of what Father John called the 'pilgrimage of meditation'. But, important as he sees this to be, he does not fail to situate it within the understanding of the experience of Christ which Father John saw lying at the heart of meditation. It is in fact John Main's theology of meditation which so excited Father Bede when he first read him. The vision is that as we pass beyond our own ego-bound consciousness of thought and imagination we move into the freedom of the mind of Christ and so find that the human consciousness of Jesus is our way to the One he called 'Father'.

The psychological and the theological are worked out and integrated, for both Father John and Father Bede, in community. The monastic community has to serve a dual function of laboratory and witness of this human journey to wholeness. Modern monasticism itself stands in need of renewal if it is to fulfil this role today. In the vision of John Main and Bede Griffiths it can achieve this renewal by re-visioning itself as the lay contemplative community movement it essentially is.

At the John Main Seminar in New Harmony, Christian meditators, who were already forming part of such a community, came together from many parts of the world to be enriched by their enjoyment of Father Bede's teaching and presence. It then naturally became the opportunity to give articulation to the international network of meditators, meditation groups and centres which continue to form out of and around the shared commitment to meditation in the tradition which John Main recovered and passed on. This was expressed as the World Community for Christian Meditation. Father Bede took part in the discussions that described its first form and structure and remained until his death in 1993 a close friend and active patron of the community.

My memory of the meeting between Father Bede and Father John focuses on a scene in a garden one sunny evening. Some light banter or teasing led to an eruption of happy laughter in which everyone shared. My more recent memory of the 1991 John Main Seminar at New Harmony also brings together sunshine and laughter. Not everyone was visibly present, but everyone who was there *was there*. Together with their wisdom this book should convey something of the warmth of Bede Griffiths and John Main who were able to share their gift of joy with each other in a way that touches us all.

This book especially and gratefully acknowledges the hospitality of Jane Owen of New Harmony, Indiana, which made the John Main Seminar of 1991 an epiphany of that spirit of unity for which New Harmony bravely stands.

Laurence Freeman, OSB

Sketched by Mary Cobb during the
John Main Seminar in New Harmony

Dom Bede Griffiths, R.I.P.

On May 13, 1993 at 4:30 p.m., Dom Bede Griffiths, O.S.B. returned to his Creator at his Ashram at Shanti-vanam, India.

A memorial mass attended by more than 1,000 persons of all faiths was celebrated at Westminster Cathedral, London, England on June 15, 1993 with a Homily in thanksgiving for the life and teaching of Bede Griffiths by Dom Laurence Freeman, monk of the Monastery of Christ the King and Teacher of the World Community for Christian Meditation (WCCM).

The WCCM was called into being by participants from around the world at the John Main Seminar held in New Harmony, Indiana in August 1991 out of the inspirational words received from the spiritual leader of this gathering, Dom Bede Griffiths, the substance of which appear in this book. Fr. Bede became a patron of the WCCM, partici-pated in the formulation of its Mission Statement and gave it his blessing:

"To communicate and nurture meditation as passed on through the teaching of John Main in the Christian tradition, in the spirit of serving the unity of all."

One of the participants at New Harmony, Mary Cobb, drew the accompanying sketch of Fr. Bede while he was sharing his wisdom with us. On receiving the news of his death, she wrote: "I had such a feeling of loss...so I listened again, to his tapes...and once more was filled with his presence — his spirit, energy, love — no more having a sense of loss — but gratefulness for his life and for his sharing his life so generously."

Milo G. Coerper

[Milo G. Coerper, the convener of the 1991 seminar, is the President of The John Main Institute, a member of the Guiding Board of the WCCM, a member of the Advisory Board of New Camaldoli Hermitage, Big Sur, California (the overseer of the Library and Archives of Dom Bede Griffiths) and an Advisor to the Bede Griffiths' Trust.]

1

The Monastic Ideal
According to John Main

St Benedict describes the monastic life as a 'search for God'. This search has gone on from the beginning of human history and it was perhaps never more intense than it is today. People everywhere are seeking for an ultimate meaning and purpose in life in a world where meaning and purpose seem to have been lost. What answer can St Benedict and the tradition which comes from him give to this problem? How can we find God in the world today? St Benedict, of course, comes from within the Christian tradition, but what answer can Christianity give? It is itself divided, and many are seeking God in other ways. Is there within the Christian tradition a path to the Supreme, not by way of doctrine or ritual but of direct experience of reality? That is what people are looking for today — not words or thoughts, but direct experience. Is there a way to the direct experience of God, of truth, of reality in the Christian tradition?

I believe that there is, and Father John Main was one of those who opened the way to this experience for people today. He found it in the Benedictine tradition stemming from the Fathers of the Desert, whose wisdom is the knowledge of God through love. Father John was a man of great wisdom and above all of great love. Let us listen to what he has to say and find for ourselves the way to this experience of God so that we can share it with the world which is waiting to hear the message and to find its way back to God. Here

14

I am drawing especially on a talk given by John Main on the witness to the world of monastic prayer.[1]

Father John begins by saying that the call of the monk, and hence of humanity as a whole — in so far as there is an archetype of the monk in every human being — is 'to be open to one's eternal potential in God, in the new creation whose centre is Christ'.[2] This shows us the way.

The idea that there is a monastic archetype in all humanity may be familiar to you from a book called *Blessed Simplicity,* edited by Father Raimundo Panikkar.[3] I think it is important to see that behind all the diversities of human nature there is a common ground and in that common ground every human being is in search of God, of ultimate meaning and ultimate truth. It is a solitary search, because it touches the depth of our being and it is something which no one else can give us. All of us human beings have a capacity for God, a capacity to be drawn by God into the depths of our being where we experience the presence of God, of the infinite, eternal reality that sustains the world as the ground and source of our being.

For many people, however, the word 'God' has lost its meaning. They do not like to use it and in fact find it embarrassing to use because it gives the wrong image to people. It is therefore helpful to get over the word and open ourselves to a deeper meaning. The particular problem here for Christians is that our concept and image of God arising from Jesus and the Gospel is primarily of the Father in heaven. Whereas when we come to the tradition of the East we find they have a different and almost opposite view. For them God is much more the ground and source of the world. A story about Father Jules Monchanin, the founder of our ashram in India, expresses the point. For many years he was a parish priest in Tannirpalli in South India. One day he approached a group of school children and asked them, 'Where is God?' The Hindu children pointed to the heart and said God was there. The Christians pointed up to the sky. These are two different ways of understanding God and of course they are complementary; we are all learning today how to reconcile opposites. Things do not have to be one thing or the other. Nearly always they are both/and, as the Chinese with their idea of *yin-yang* knew. Everything is interrelated. So when we think of God we do need images but we need the image both of the Father in heaven and of the Holy Spirit within us.

This experience of God is not something that requires any special learning or ability. It is something that exists at the very centre of our being which gives meaning and purpose to our existence and which alone can answer the deepest need of human life. At our ashram we see people coming from all five continents and it is almost uncanny to find that they are all seeking for the same thing. They are all trying to find a deeper meaning in life, a deeper self, a deeper relation to God and to humanity. They are, as we often say in India, trying to 'realize God'. For most people this capacity for depth has been almost lost. It has been so obscured that they are no longer aware of it. Particularly in the materialistic civilization in the West, people have lost this dimension from their lives. They are so occupied with the world around them and so absorbed in its problems, pleasures and pains, that they do not have the power to get beyond. They have lost the sense of being open to God, to the transcendent. Father John said this when he remarked that we are trying to recover the sense of God which modern culture has obscured.

All the meditation groups throughout the world are composed of people searching for this deeper meaning in their lives. Father John refers to this movement to recover our capacity for God as the 'new creation'. This capacity, innate in every human being, has been obscured through sin, that is, through alienation from one's own true being. Sin is alienation. It is failing to know oneself as one really is and so falling into illusion. Alienation from one's self, from reality and from God calls for the new creation. This is the renewal of our being which takes place when we awake to who we are, to the reality behind all the superficial appearances of our life. In India the question is often asked, 'Who am I? Am I this body sitting here?

Am I this personality relating to other people? Or is there something deeper within, beyond my body and my mind? Is there a deeper reality in me?' As Father John says,

> ...the new creation is a passing beyond all the illusions and images which we project of ourselves and the world around us and discovering our true being, our inner self, which has been hidden behind all these illusory appearances.[4]

Every human being tends to get lost in this world of appearances, of illusion, and to lose sight of the reality behind it all.

Father John sees the monastic life, that is the life of the monk hidden within everyone, as a way of transcendence. Karl Rahner described a human being as a being 'constituted by the capacity for self-transcendence'. We have fallen into a separated self, shut out from others and from the ground and source of our own being. We have to transcend this separated self, this ego which hides our true being, and open ourselves to God and the world, to the life and the truth which are everywhere and in every person. This separated self is the source of all evil. It is not that the ego is evil in itself. We have to have an ego, a separate self. A child has to grow and become aware of itself. It has to separate from the mother and become a person. But we get shut up in the ego, and this shuts us out from others and from God and imprisons us. To some degree we are all imprisoned in the separate self. The grace of God received in prayer and meditation is the way to go beyond the ego.

The way of transcendence, of course, is the way of love. To love, as Father John says, is 'to turn beyond self to another'.[5] That is why he speaks of an 'infinite expansion of spirit'.[6] To love is to expand oneself, to open oneself to the infinity of being which is in us and around us, and this infinity of being in love is what we mean by God. This in turn leads to a 'creative development of our whole being, a deepening of the integral harmony of heart and mind'.[7] We need to think of ourselves always as an integrated whole body and soul and spirit. Unfortunately, we have become used to thinking of the human being as a rational animal, body-soul. This is all right as far as it goes, but it leaves out the deeper dimension of our being. St Paul and the early Church always thought of the human being as body, soul and spirit. When we pray, when we meditate, we are not doing so only in the mind. Because of our Western prejudice of excessively educating the mind, we are in danger of our religion being only in the head. Meditation should be a way of bringing it down from the head into the heart. The Fathers used to say, 'Bring the thoughts from the head into the heart and keep them there.' The heart is the centre where the head joins the rest of the body and so, in taking us from head to heart, our meditation involves and renews our whole being.

We begin to see now what is the meaning of a 'new creation'. It is to transcend the separated self with its illusory images and desires and to encounter reality, the reality of our own being and of the world in which we live. It may sound very easy to encounter reality but it is prevented by the images which we project. Scientists today tell us that the entire three-dimensional world is all a projection. The world is a field of energies vibrating at different frequencies, and within that field there are various structures or forms which we interpret as a three-dimensional universe. But this universe is a projection and so, in a sense, an illusory appearance behind which is reality. Prayer, meditation, is the way to get beyond the appearances and to touch the reality. The reality is God who is always revealing himself behind all appearances.

Transcendence of illusion is a way of love, of going beyond our separate self and opening ourself to others. We go to that communion of love in which the real meaning of human existence is to be found and which is, as far as we know, the nature of God. John Main describes this reality as the 'mutual love which is God'.[8] If God is mutual love we must be careful how we project an image of God, which too often is much as we project the world around us. Most of us have an image of God as a person, but in the Christian

18

tradition God is not 'a' person. God is interpersonal communion, a communion of love which is in all of us and embraces us all as the real meaning of our lives.

This is the other aspect of our 'infinite potential in God'. We know the nature of God as love through its revelation in Christ. In India the search for God has led to the discovery of the true Self, the ground of human existence, the supreme reality. In the fifth century before Christ the Upanishads described the breakthrough beyond the world of appearances, of the senses and the mind, to the true Self or Atman, as they call it. People all over the world today are searching to realize the Self and to discover their true being and the reality of the world, by the methods of meditation and yoga. Some Christians are prejudiced against yoga, even against medita-tion, but they are learning that these are valid methods tested over thousands of years to help us discover God. There are many methods of meditation and ways of life today. Yoga, Zen, *vipassana* and transcendental meditation have all had a wide influence and seek to open and reveal the inner meaning of life and the purpose of life in the world. But the monastic life, as Father John saw it, is essentially a way of love. All of these methods have their particular value and insights, but the particular Christian way that Father John discovered is this way of love. He saw the way of love as a way of sharing with others, and this is why he saw meditation as a way of opening oneself to others. The danger of meditation is that it can shut oneself up. As Father John saw it, it is a way of opening; if you open yourself to God then you also open up to others.

In one of his books Father John speaks of the 'Community of Love'. He always saw meditation as leading to community, and this insight is a very important one for us today. He gives the beautiful example of St Aelred, the abbot of the Cistercian abbey of Rievaulx in England in the twelfth century. St Aelred writes,

The day before yesterday as I was walking around the cloister of the monastery, the brethren were sitting around forming as it were a most loving crown. In the multitude I found no one whom I did not love and by whom I felt sure I was not loved. I was filled with such joy that it surpassed all the delights of the world. I felt my spirit transfused into all and the affection of all to have passed into me, so that I could say with the prophet: Behold how good and pleasant it is for brothers to dwell together in unity.[9]

How did St Aelred and his brother monks reach this extraordinary degree of love? That is what we have to ask ourselves when we think of community life today. I believe that Father John had an answer. It was in their prayer. Father John had experienced this love, and he taught a method of prayer which he believed could lead others to the same experience.

We are trying to find a way of living together in love. And it is very difficult: how many marriages break up a few years after people have gone into marriage full of love and in the hope of it lasting a lifetime! Something is destroying love, and we are trying to find the way Christ has revealed to us to live together in love again. Our meditation has to lead us to that love. If it does not lead to this *agape* — Christian love which is self-giving and self-sacrificing — it is not fulfilling its purpose.

The method of prayer which Father John discovered was that of Cassian and the Fathers of the Desert of the fourth century, who were the guides of St Benedict. Cassian was a monk who came from what is now Yugoslavia and travelled to visit the monks of the desert in Egypt. In the fourth century Egypt was full of Christian monks who had left the society of the Roman empire to search for God in the solitude of the desert. Cassian interviewed these monks and wrote his *Conferences*[10] describing their life and particularly their way of prayer. The two Conferences of Abbot Isaac on Prayer are a classical teaching on the whole subject of meditation. The Rule of St Benedict derives its teaching on prayer from Cassian and the Desert Fathers. This is what Father John, in his monastery twenty years ago, discovered in Cassian.

This prayer, without words or thought, is the secret of prayer which Father John recovered for us. This can be quite a problem for many people, who think of words and thoughts when they think of prayer. Such thinking and talking is of course needed to begin, but prayer has to lead to that point beyond the thinking and talking mind which Evagrius, one of the great monks of the desert, calls 'pure prayer'. St Benedict mentions purity of heart as the quality of prayer and it is this which we are all seeking. I myself lived in a Benedictine monastery for twenty years and never discovered it! We used to meditate for half an hour after Vespers but we were given no instruction or guidance in it. This is what people are looking for today. The popularity of the Russian classic *The Way of a Pilgrim*[11] suggests how seriously people are seeking the kind of practical wisdom on prayer, which the Pilgrim sought and found from the *staretz* who taught him to say the Jesus Prayer without ceasing. Nineteenth-century Russia was 'holy Russia', and pilgrims wandered all over the country between monasteries and churches searching for God and worshipping God. The Pilgrim transformed his life and radiated Christ once he had found the Prayer. As the old Communist system is breaking up in Russia today people there are once again rediscovering their soul.

We are more accustomed to pray with words and concepts and, of course, these are necessary to begin with. A traditional way of monastic prayer is *lectio divina,* the meditative reading of the Bible. This is an excellent practice and fundamental, but it hardly goes beyond discursive prayer, taking us as it does from thought to thought. It may be a way to contemplation but it is not yet properly contemplative prayer. Contemplative prayer begins when all discursive thought ceases, and when the mind rests in silence in the presence of God. Contemplation is the practice of the presence of God, and the mantra, the repetition of a sacred word, takes us into the silence of that presence. What we have to ask now is, what is the nature of this prayer and how has it the power to transform our lives?

Father John gives the answer when he speaks of 'transcendence in union'.[12] We have first of all to transcend ourselves, to go beyond our ego, our senses and mind, and enter into the silence, the stillness, the inward depth of our being. When we sit quietly in meditation, this is what we are trying to do. But then we have to go out of ourselves in love. It is here that we touch the heart of Christian prayer and meditation. Many oriental traditions teach this way of transcendence, to go beyond the ego, sense and mind, and to become aware of the transcendent mystery of being, known in Hinduism as Brahman or Atman. For many people in the West today, who do not believe in God or Christ, the way to find the depths of their being is through yoga in the Indian way.

The next stage, though, is to open our hearts in love to this transcendent reality and to find the mystery of love at the heart of our being. That is our particular Christian calling. For the Hindu this is the way of *bhakti,* of devotion to a personal God. But the danger in this is that God is normally represented in human form as Rama, Krishna, Siva or some other god or goddess. The mystery of God tends to be limited once it is given a particular personal form, whether it is the guru or a god. There is a similar danger for Christians in focusing excessively on the human nature of Jesus, in what the fathers called the 'anthropomorphic blasphemy'.[13] St Paul says, 'If we knew Jesus once after the manner of the flesh we know him so no more.'[14] According to the flesh, means knowing him simply as a human being, a great prophet or holy man but no more. This way we fail to recognize God in Christ. We have to go through Jesus in his humanity to the Father, through the human to the divine. Jesus is always taking us to the Father, particularly as he is described in St John's gospel. Here he says that the Son has no authority of himself, that he can do nothing unless he is obeying the Father. Jesus is from the Father and to the Father. The Father is the Origin, the Source, the One beyond name and form. Jesus gives him name and form but the Father himself is what in India is call *arupa,* without name or form. Jesus reveals the Father as a source of infinite love, which he shares with the Father. It is the goal of Christian meditation, as Father John said, 'to share in the stream of love which flows between Jesus and the Father and is the Holy Spirit'.[15]

Christian meditation consists in entering into this 'stream of love' in the intimacy of a personal union with the persons of the Trinity. Meditation leads us to that depth where the Holy Spirit is present and takes us into the inner mystery of God's life and love. The persons of the Trinity are 'subsistent relations' in which Being expresses and communicates itself in love. The Father expresses himself in his Word. The Word is the self-expression of the Father who communicates himself in the Spirit. The Father knows and loves the Son, and that knowledge and love of the Father and the Son is the Holy Spirit. It is mutual love. This is the end of our human quest, to experience love in its ultimate depth in interpersonal communion.

This is also the 'experience of God' which we have to seek, to transcend ourselves in a total self-giving in love and find ourselves taken up into an ocean of love, which is at once deeply personal and at the same time transcends all human limitations. This answers our fundamental need of love. For most people it is their interpersonal relationships which are the main features of their lives, whether as husband, wife, son, daughter, friend or associate. It is these relationships which make up the reality of their lives. God himself is this relationship of love, and our relationships are a faint reflection of that love which is eternal in God as the Father, the Son and the Holy Spirit. It is what Father John calls 'the movement of transcendence right beyond ourselves, and into the life of the Trinity, the communion of God, the mutual love which is God'.[16] The life of the Trinity is the mutual love which is God.

It only remains to add that this love embraces our whole being, body, soul and spirit. The love which begins with a child's love for ts mother or of the mother for the child and goes through all the stages of adolescent and married love and opens on to the love of friendship, uniting all human beings in love, as St Aelred described it, is a love which creates of our divided humanity a new Man, a new creation, a mystical body, in which the human and divine meet in one.

To end this chapter here is a quotation from St Paul's Letter to the Ephesians. It is my favourite expression of Christian meditation.

> For this cause I bow my knees to the Father, from whom all fatherhood in heaven and earth takes its name. I pray that according to the riches of his glory, he may grant you to be strengthened in your inner being with power through the Spirit, that Christ may dwell in your hearts through faith, as you are being rooted and grounded in love, and that you may know with all the saints what is the height, the depth, the length and the breadth, and may know the love of Christ which surpasses knowledge and be filled with the fullness of God.[17]

1 John Main, *Community of Love*, Darton Longman and Todd 1990.
2 Ibid., 'The Monastic Adventure'.
3 R. Panikkar et al., *Blessed Simplicity*, Harper and Row 1982.
4 John Main, *Community of Love*, 'The Monastic Adventure'.
5 Ibid.
6 Ibid.
7 Ibid.
8 Ibid.
9 Ibid., 'Monastic Prayer Today'.
10 *John Cassian: Conferences*, tr. Colm Luibheid, Paulist Press 1985.
11 R.M. French (ed.), *The Way of a Pilgrim*, SPCK 1972.
12 John Main, *Community of Love*, 'The Monastic Adventure'
13 Ibid., 'Monastic Prayer Today' (quoting Cassian).
14 2 Corinthians 5:16.
15 John Main, *Community of Love*, 'The Monastic Adventure'.
16 Ibid.
17 Ephesians 3:14-19.

2

The Extension of the Monastic Ideal to the Laity

In the Benedictine tradition, as I experienced it in England in the first half of this century, there was no method of meditation. We were left to ourselves. St Benedict structured monastic prayer around the Divine Office: the seven hours of communal and vocal prayer during the day, beginning with the night office in the early hours of morning. It is true that the chanting of the Divine Office in Gregorian Chant had a deeply contemplative character and could lead to contemplation, but it was not itself a strictly contemplative prayer. During the twenty years I was in Prinknash Abbey chanting the Latin office was a wonderful experience, deeply contemplative in spirit if not in form. I am always grateful for it. In the same way, a monk's *lectio divina,* meditating on the sacred scriptures could lead to true contemplation, but again, it is not properly contemplative insofar as it is a method of meditation with words and thoughts that can easily be distracting, whereas pure prayer is prayer beyond words, beyond thoughts.

Of course, the Benedictine tradition has not been closed to change. I might mention, for example, Augustine Baker, an English Benedictine monk of the sixteenth century. Augustine Baker and his contemporary, Blosius (Louis de Blois) developed a profound method of contemplative prayer under the influence of St Teresa of Avila and St John of the Cross; and this had a considerable influence until quite recently. But it was a way of prayer that was extremely individualistic and ascetic. It tended to exclude the ordinary person from contemplation and make it appear, as it has long been considered, an exclusive way of prayer for a few chosen souls. That has been the problem for the last two or three centuries. Contemplative prayer has been thought to be the domain of monks and nuns, chosen people living a particular way of life, and out of the reach of lay people working in the world. The great change that is taking place today is the discovery that contemplation is open to everyone.

We must not forget that we have had in our Catholic tradition a strong tendency to extreme asceticism. The Fathers of the Desert used to rival one another as to how long they could fast, how long they could stay up at night, whether they could say the whole Psalter every day, and so on. It was a fervour of youth. St Benedict moderated it a great deal. But nonetheless we have had a negative view of 'the world and the flesh'. Of course, there is some biblical basis for this, but we are learning that although 'the world and the flesh' can present temptations, they also have their own value. The Second Vatican Council, in the Constitution on the Church in the Modern World, was responsible for helping us realize the values of the secular life in the world today. We have seen how in Eastern Europe, freedom and democracy have taken hold of whole populations. And these, of course, are secular ideals.

We recognize today the value of the world and the value of the flesh, the body. The 'flesh', narrowly understood, can have a negative connotation, but the body is sacred. In the letter to the Corinthians, St Paul says, 'Your body is the temple of the Holy Spirit.' The body is sacred. We are learning to appreciate the physical self, particularly through yoga, which is coming into general use more and more. It is a way of harmonizing the body and learning to live in it. There is a great danger of living only in your mind, in your head, and neglecting your body or the other senses. That has created a negative attitude toward the body, to the senses, to the outer world.

A famous example of Christian asceticism is Thomas à Kempis' *Imitation of Christ,* which was extremely popular for nearly five hundred years. But it is now seen as a limited and negative form of spirituality. It is not a good model today. We are trying to realize the importance of both body and soul. The body is part of the whole physical organism of nature: the whole earth, the whole planet, the stars and the stellar universe. It is a whole in which we share. We are learning to experience the body as sacred. The Word became flesh. God entered into this human, concrete, fleshly existence and gave us his flesh and his blood to eat and to drink. That is a tremendous reversal of negative asceticism. We are trying to learn to appreciate the body and the world, and to integrate them into our Christian lives. I think this is very important.

The person responsible for bringing Christian contemplative life to lay people was Father John Main. It was a wonderful achievement, a great gift of God for the Church. He found a method of meditation in the *Conferences* of Cassian, a monk of the fifth century, who visited the Fathers of the Desert in their solitude and described their way of life and prayer. Cassian spoke of 'pure prayer' as a way of meditation, using a short word or verse repeated continually in order to avoid distractions and to attain 'purity of heart'. He gives the example, 'God, come to my aid. Lord, make haste to help me.' That was the earliest Christian mantra. Whatever the situation, whenever anything unexpected happened or any danger arose, 'God, come to my aid. Lord, make haste to help me,' was the guide in life. Different verses from the Psalms or other parts of the Bible were also used. In the 'Jesus Prayer', which became the norm of this kind of prayer in the Eastern Church, one repeated constantly, 'Lord Jesus Christ, Son of God, have mercy on me a sinner.' That is another ancient and characteristic Christian mantra.

In reintroducing 'pure prayer', Father John chose the mantra 'Maranatha' (Aramaic for 'Lord, come'). This is important because Jesus spoke Aramaic. Since our gospels are written in Greek, no words that Jesus actually spoke in his own language are recorded. To be precise there are just six words. In Mark 5:41 when Jesus raises a little girl, he is quoted as saying, 'Talitha cumi' ('Little girl,

I say to you, arise.') And on the cross, as reported in Mark 15:34 and Matthew 27:46, Jesus is heard to say, 'Eloi, Eloi, lama sabachthani' ('My God, My God, why have you forsaken me?'). Other than these words, everything that Jesus said is translated into Greek. 'Maranatha' occurs in the First Letter of Paul to the Corinthians[1] and was used in the early Church as one of the relics of Aramaic, Jesus' own speech. That is why it is a very sacred word. When for ten years I was a member of the Syrian Church in Kerala, we learned Syriac which is virtually the same language as the Aramaic spoken by Jesus and the apostles. When we use 'Maranatha', it takes us back to the time of Jesus himself.

The idea of 'prayer without ceasing' was again taken up in the West, in the fourteenth century, in a book called *The Cloud of Unknowing*, which has had a tremendous influence on so many people today. It is a medieval classic written by an unknown author, probably a priest, in beautiful, simple and direct English. The author suggests taking one word, 'God' or 'Love', and repeating it silently. As a whole, the book is a beautiful presentation of contemplative prayer. This, like the work of Cassian and the 'Jesus prayer', is part of the tradition that Father John rediscovered and reclaimed for the ordinary Christian. He devoted his life to spreading the availability of 'pure prayer' throughout the modern Church, thus opening the way of contemplation to lay people as well as to monks and nuns. This is really a breakthrough, a new movement in the Church. As is clear, the Church today is moving towards the recognition of the laity, and this rediscovery and reclamation of an ancient tradition is part of the larger movement of the Church of the Laity. You probably know that the word 'laity' comes from the Greek *laos,* which means 'people', the people of God. Father John has made it possible for the people of God to share in the deep life of prayer, the inner prayer of the Spirit.

We should remind ourselves that Father John originally learned this way of prayer with a mantra from a Hindu swami whom he met in Malaya before he became a Benedictine monk. This is important.

As we have seen, we have our own Christian tradition of prayer with a mantra that can be traced back to the Fathers of the Desert, but we must also remember that it links us with a tradition of prayer from the earliest times in the East, particularly in India. It is important that we see our Christian meditation as part of a whole movement of meditation — Hindu and Buddhist, Jain and Sikh, Moslem and Sufi — spreading throughout the world. We place ourselves within that movement. Father John made the link when he learned prayer with a mantra from a Hindu swami.

The value of this method is that it simplifies prayer and reduces it to its fundamental ground in the depths of the soul. The problem with the Divine Office, which many devout Catholics used to recite, is that it consists of too *many* psalms, each day's selection takes a long time to say, and not many people are able to enter into all of its imagery. It is not suited to lay life, but the mantra is perfectly suited to everybody. It is simple. It reduces prayer to its basis. It releases one from the endless distractions of the mind and integrates the whole person into its deepest centre. It can be described as the practice of the presence of God. That is my favourite phrase.

There is a beautiful little book called *The Practice of the Presence of God* by Brother Lawrence. He spent most of his life working in the kitchen and going to market. The kitchen must be one of the most distracting places in the world, yet he learned the presence of God there. Oddly enough, reciting some parts of the Divine Office can be even more distracting than working in the kitchen. For anyone acquainted with modern biblical criticism, as we need to be, many of the psalms can be seen to belong to a primitive stage of religion when the people of God were still learning to transcend their image of a God of wrath and vengeance, and only beginning to discover the face of a God of infinite mercy and grace. This problem of the psalms is becoming acute.

In the early Church and even right up to recent times, many teachers and scholars had a wonderful *symbolic* understanding of the Old Testament. St Gregory the Great on the Book of Job is a perfect example. One is often awed by the meanings the Fathers read into the Hebrew Bible and their capacity for absorbing the negative aspects of it into their Christian faith. But today it is virtually impossible to overlook the literal and historical connotations of biblical language. So I think we need to revise the Psalter. We have to omit some psalms and some verses because they are really scandalous. For example, 'Do I not hate those that hate you? Yes, I hate them.' We have to learn to go beyond that. Jesus was taking us beyond the Old Testament. The messianic psalms (Psalms 2 and 110) are among the most offensive. Psalm 2 says of the Messiah 'He shall break them in pieces like a potter's vessel.' In Psalm 110 it is said: 'He shall heap high the corpses.' When he died on the cross Jesus was taking us beyond that symbol of the conquering king of Israel to the figure of the suffering servant. This is a total reversal of the old concept of the Messiah. So we have to learn to read the psalms with more discrimination. Things begin in a simple, often crude, way and gradually evolve into something deeper and more meaningful. The Bible is the history of humanity in its growth from primitive beginnings to the fullness of life and truth.

Father John's great insight was that the Divine Office could be a preparation for contemplative prayer and also an overflow from our contemplation, *but that it needed to lead to pure prayer*. This is to change the focus of Christian prayer from the Divine Office, the prayer of monks and religious, to the pure prayer of self-surrender in love. That is the essence of this way which is open to every Christian. I think it is a message for monks as well. In our ashram we have spontaneously moved to placing the two hours of meditation, morning and evening, at the centre of our lives. In India, the early hours are considered the best time for meditation, and the time of sundown: they call it 'the meeting of the light and the darkness'. In all Hindu ashrams you meditate morning and evening at those times. In our ashram we normally meet between half past five and half past six in the morning, and six and seven in the evening. Many come to sit by the river. We all take our time then to meditate. That is the focus of the day. Then we go to church, we have our communal prayer, we have our Mass, and we share together. It is a kind of overflow from meditation and also a nourishment you take in at that time from the readings and prayers. You open your heart. For me, the focus has changed; it is now on pure prayer, contemplative prayer, and the divine office is an overflow from it.

I think this is where Father John is leading us: to introducing monastic prayer to lay people, but also to deepening the prayer of the monks and nuns so that they can enter into the silence and solitude of being 'alone with God' while they keep open to the Church and humanity through participation in the Divine Office. So it works both ways. The monk opens to the lay people and shares with them and lay people discover a deeper way of prayer. The fundamental insight of Father John was that this pure prayer of meditation could be shared with people outside the monastery.

Most of you probably know the story of how this came to pass. When Father John was a monk at Ealing Abbey near London, as is recorded in his *Letters from the Heart*,[2] a small group of lay people began to come to the monastery to meditate. This grew spontaneously into a regular movement of the Spirit, drawing more and more people to meditate with a mantra, as Father John taught them, and to begin a regular practice of meditation in their homes. It was apparently quite dramatic! As the group gathered and began to meditate, more people came, and started meditating at home as well. They felt that the Holy Spirit was driving them. It was quite extraordinary.

Eventually, Father John was invited to open a house of prayer in Montreal, Canada, where monks and lay people could live together and share their way of meditation with others. This led to the growth of meditation groups under the guidance of Father Laurence Freeman (who accompanied Father John to Montreal and carried on Father John's work after he died) and the practice has now spread to hundreds of groups of oblates of St Benedict throughout the world. An oblate of St Benedict is usually a lay person (though priests may also join), man or woman, married or single, who dedicates his or her life to following the Rule of St Benedict in its basic principles, especially the pattern of prayer and work, *ora et labora,* centred on the service of God. In former times, this prayer was based on the Divine Office, but now it is based on the mantra. That is a great change. Father John's inspiration was to reclaim an ancient form of meditation that could be practised by anyone who is prepared to give up half an hour every morning and evening in a single-hearted devotion to God alone, even in the midst of the distractions of daily life. You withdraw from ordinary life and are enriched to go back to it with more meaning, more under-standing and more purpose. This way of praying leads to the experience of God in love. It is always the discovery of God in love which is the end of meditation.

We should not forget, by the way, that St Francis of Sales, through his preaching and his book on *The Devout Life,* spread the message of the love of God to lay people in the seventeenth century. It was very famous and his form of devotion has had a wide influence. But, in my opinion, Father John's simple and direct method of meditation is better suited to the needs of lay people in the twentieth century.

The next stage of the movement is only now beginning. Medi-tation groups in which people meet once or more times a week are beginning to grow into regular oblate communities. Father John's attempt to combine regular monastic life with oblates in one com-munity has not proved successful. It seems clear that the two vocations have to be linked but separate. The break-up of the community in Montreal was a tragedy, in a way, but I think it has a lesson for us all: that you cannot combine monastic life and lay life in one group. Monks must have their way of life, which is valid and true for them, and lay people must find their own way. What we are trying now is to find how lay people can live together and share their prayer. The monk has a special calling to live out a life of prayer in a regular community. The oblate is a lay person, married or single, living a normal life in the world, but feeling a call to form a community of some kind with others of like mind dedicated to the service of God in prayer and meditation.

This is a growing movement throughout the world. Meditation groups practising yoga and zen, *vipassana* and other Eastern methods of meditation are springing up everywhere in Europe, America, Asia, Australia, and South Africa. I am in touch with groups all over the world. Recently I spent some time in California at the Empty Gate Zen Centre. Zen is not my method. It is a different approach, but it has its own value. A group of young people meet together to meditate within a strict discipline. Zen is very strict. They do prostrations, chants, and, of course, they meditate in silence. Their lives are centred on contemplation. We call it the experience of the inner life, the inner reality.

The growth of oblate communities dedicated to meditation in the Christian tradition is part of the world movement. Father John's gift to the Church is the renewal of this tradition with the goal of transforming Christian life. I think we must go back to that. So often, one person can change life for thousands or millions. So often, one person must break through and then everything else follows from that. It should be noted that a similar method of 'centering prayer', developed at the Trappist Abbey in Spencer, Massachusetts, is another branch of the same tradition with only slight differences in the actual practice. It has its own distinctive character, but they are parallel movements, and equally valid.

I have been much impressed in America by the number of people who are looking for community. There is a vast number who feel a call to give their lives to God, but not in a monastery or convent and not simply in an isolated secular family. They want what we could call a 'dedicated' secular life. I think the Church and the Holy Spirit are raising up these lay communities as a new way of Christian life.

It is good to remember that Father John's teaching reaches back not simply to the Desert Fathers, but to Jesus himself in the New Testament. One of the great insights in New Testament scholarship is that Jesus' whole life is centred on his '*Abba* experience'. Jesus referred to God as *Abba,* an intimate way of speaking of 'Father', more like 'Daddy'. A child calls his father *Abba,* as he or she calls her mother *Mamma.* Jesus had an intimate relation with God as Father, whereas the Jews of the Old Testament had the opposite. Yahweh was the God of heaven, and their reverence was so great that they did not even like to name him. *Adonai* or Lord was substituted for Yahweh because it was forbidden to name God. He was so far above the human that there was the fear of judgement and a sense that the Law had to be kept at all costs. Jesus went right beyond that to an intimate awareness of his total oneness with *Abba,* his Father. I think you could say that *Abba* was Jesus' mantra. He simply lived in that intimacy with the Father. And so from him we gain the tradition of the mantra.

On that word, with all it implied, Jesus' whole life centred. When a Christian invokes the name of Jesus, he or she is entering into the prayer of Jesus. This was another insight of Father John's: to enter into the prayer of Jesus is to share his intimate life with the Father in the mystery of the Godhead. It is important, therefore, that oblates of St Benedict should keep in touch with a monastery of men or women where the Christian tradition of prayer is preserved. I think we all recognize this. Groups are scattered about every-where, but they need some link with a tradition. Father John always spoke of the 'tradition'. It is a living thing that goes from person to person and we need that connection. The oblate can draw on the riches of the tradition preserved in the monastic life and the monks can learn from their association with oblates to realize how this prayer can become a vital force in the world. That is what we are looking for.

In our ashram at Shantivanam we have a continual flow of visitors from all over the world, all in search of God, looking for a way of prayer and meditation that will enable them to discover their true selves, to integrate their personality, and to relate to the Church in a new and significant way. It is a bit saddening to see the number of people who simply leave the Church today because they cannot find the kind of prayer they are looking for. I cannot say how many, but I get the impression that 60 per cent of the Catholics who come to our ashram are no longer practising. They do not go to Mass any more and yet they are searching for God, and they come to Shantivanam to learn how to come closer to God. I think there are many reasons for this that involve the Church as a whole, but people are discovering that when they get into the prayer of the mantra, it takes them back to their faith. Many Catholics come to the ashram who are no longer attending Mass and, after some weeks, they spontaneously come back to Communion, to reading the Bible, to discovering the Church from *within*.

If you look at the Church from without, you can easily become alienated. When you learn to see what is behind the Mass, what is behind the Church, the Reality of Christ, then of course your whole life changes. That is what we have to help people to do, to see the inner mystery of the Church, behind the outer forms. Many who have given up the practice of their faith seek a more authentic life. Some go to Buddhist monasteries, Hindu ashrams, to Sufis, but many, after some experience, recover their roots, as they say. After a time, they begin to feel that they have lost something, and they come back. Innumerable people go out first of all to rediscover God. In their experience of prayer in our ashram, they often recover their faith and are able to see the Church in a new light, no longer from without but from within. It is to a renewal of Christian life and the recovery of the deeper reality of the Church that our meditation must lead us.

The question remains: how to organize lay communities in which the focus will always be on prayer and meditation? That is the centre. Normally there will be prayer and meditation in the morning and evening, and some simple ritual. At Shantivanam we begin with Sanskrit chanting. As I mentioned before, a sacred language has a powerful character. Latin had it, Greek still has it, and I think Old Slavonic has it. Sanskrit, above all perhaps, is a sacred language. It opens you up to the world of the sacred. So we normally begin with Sanskrit chanting, then we read from the Upanishads or the Bhagavadgita or one of the Hindu classics.

In reading these texts, we get in touch not only with the sacred but also with a world movement. In the fifth century before Christ, there was a breakthrough in human history. Carl Jaspers called it the 'axial period'. Something happened that enabled humanity to break through the world of the senses, the outer world with all its gods and goddesses, to the realization of infinite transcendent reality and truth. One sees it in the Upanishads, in the Buddha in India, in Lao Tsu in China, and, to some extent, in Zarathustra in Persia, in Greece with Heraclitus, Socrates, and Plato, and, at the same time, in Israel with the major prophets. It was a worldwide phenomenon. All the main religions of the world stem from that time. That is where we have our common roots. To begin one's prayer and meditation by linking with this breakthrough of humanity is important.

Of course, for the lay person, this focus on prayer and meditation has to be integrated into a normal existence while earning a living in the world. That is where the problems begin. And that is what we have to work on. Such a life can involve various occupations such as the cultivation of music, art, science and philosophy. One community may be involved in research into academic questions, another in the composition and performance of music. Yet another might dedicate itself to the care of those in need. For example, Jean Vanier and the L'Arche communities that he founded to care for the mentally handicapped. Though the handicapped are often despised and rejected as less than human, Jean Vanier has found in them a great longing and capacity for love. When they are given love, they are transformed. It changes their lives.

Lay communities can also work with AIDS patients, the mentally ill and prisoners. When you know that you are going to die, it sets your sights in a new direction. If people can learn that illness is not a punishment for their sins, but an opening on God and eternal life, they can make their disease a means for tremendous growth in grace. Another lay apostolate is to prisoners. It can open up the lives of the imprisoned so that they can see that they are not simply rejected. There is a good book written on this subject entitled *We Are All Doing Time*.[3] I was in touch with a prisoner once who told me that people had been trying to help him for years, but nothing happened until he began meditating. In a few months, his life was changed. He discovered the value of solitude, nothing to do, nothing to read; it was a wonderful opportunity to be alone with God. You can find God in your prison cell. There is great opportunity there.

All these are ways in which a meditation group can move out to help others and to be immensely helped by them. One of the things being discovered is that you go out to help the mentally handicapped or sick or imprisoned, and you find out how much *they help you*. Again and again, people in L'Arche communities tell me, 'We learn far more than they do. They teach us how to be human.'

Given all that is happening in Russia and Eastern Europe, I should also mention the immense opportunities emerging there. People are entering into prayer groups and thirsting for the knowledge of God which they have been deprived of for so long. Jean Vanier has said, that when he recently gave a talk in Moscow, he ended it with a meditation and the silence was profound. The people there have been starved for love. There is a great opportunity to bring lay groups, the lay life of contemplative communities into Eastern Europe and Russia.

Finally, we have to think of how to connect all the lay communities around the world. We all feel we should have a network. We do not want a big organization. That is a great danger. We must have some kind of centre, but the federation should be loose so that each community can maintain its own individuality, with its own customs and traditions, and yet be linked with the others and with a monastery or spiritual guide. That seems to be the pattern to which we should look. When you have a small community (and they should normally be small) other people can come and after a while hive off and start another, rather than let any single group grow too large. Big communities always create problems, economic problems, first of all.

But whatever the organization, we must always remember that these groups are essentially contemplative. We must never let go of that. Otherwise we are going to lose the real value and meaning. Whatever the work to be done, whatever service we do, it must be related and intimately associated with our prayer, our meditation, our contemplation. We are trying to bring our whole life, our whole being, our secular life, into this inner life of prayer. That is what we are seeking. That is our hope for these lay communities. And this is our prayer: that all these groups and meetings taking place will gradually evolve into a new kind of church, a church that is focused on contemplative prayer, renewing the whole Christian life and, we hope, human life in the context of prayer.

1 1 Corinthians 16:22.
2 John Main, *Letters from the Heart,* Crossroad Pub. Co. 1983.
3 Bo Lozoff, *We Are All Doing Time,* Human Kindness Foundation   3rd edn. 1989.

3

The Way of Meditation with a Mantra

We come now to the heart of Father John's method of meditation, the use of a mantra. We must remember that 'mantra' is a Sanskrit word and derives from a long tradition of prayer and meditation in India. It was the genius of Father John which discovered the same tradition in the Fathers of the Desert and saw it as a sacred tradition which had come to St Benedict from the fathers and had been preserved, though almost lost, in the Benedictine Order today. He was the first to bring the mantra to light and make it known as a valid method of prayer in the Church of today. The art of the mantra consists in the repetition of a sacred word or a verse from the Bible, which has the effect of 'centering' the person, unifying all the faculties and focusing them on the indwelling presence of God. The same discovery was made in Spencer Abbey under the influence of the Maharishi's Transcendental Meditation and led to the concept of 'centering prayer'.[1]

The mantra is a method of centering oneself, of finding the inner centre of one's being and bringing all the faculties of sense and reason to unite in this centre and so open the depths of the human person to the indwelling presence of God. Father John chose as his mantra the Aramaic word *Maranatha,* which can be translated as either 'Come Lord' or, probably more correctly, 'Our Lord comes', or 'the Lord is coming', and is from St Paul's Letter to the Corinthians.[2] For those interested in the Aramaic the word *Mar* simply means 'Lord', and bishops in Kerala are called Mar Athanasius, Mar Theophilus and so on. The suffix *-an* means 'our' so *maran* really means 'Our Lord'. It is one of the very few Aramaic words — the language of Jesus himself — which have survived in the New Testament. It takes us back, therefore, beyond the New Testament itself, which was written in Greek, to the earliest tradition of the Church before it had emerged from its Jewish matrix.

We must remember that the New Testament came into being over a period of about fifty years after Jesus and that it was a translation into Greek of the original story. We do not therefore know Jesus' own words. It is deeply significant that he left no words behind him. If he had, we would have idolized them. Instead, he left it to the Holy Spirit to lead his disciples to translate his teaching and pass it on. Early Christianity grew up in a Jewish world. Jesus and his disciples spoke Aramaic, worshipped in the Temple and preached in the synagogue. Then in the course of the first century Christianity began to move into the Gentile world, largely under the influence of Paul. Paul was a Greek-speaking Jew from Tarsus who carried this message to the Gentiles. His letters were written in Greek and so the whole message of Jesus was transmitted through Greek to the quite different culture of the Greco-Roman world. This meeting of two cultures is of great significance.

There is, incidentally, a story, supposedly contained in a manuscript in a Tibetan monastery, that Jesus went to India and to the Himalayas and preached the Gospel there between the ages of twelve and thirty. The legend has no foundation in history, and personally I believe that Jesus belonged only to the Jewish world and came through a particular Jewish culture which had been prepared by God over the centuries. The Gospel grew up in that Jewish world, and in the course of the first century it grew beyond it, into the Greco-Roman world. Then it passed into Europe and eventually into America. At the same time it moved eastwards to Syria, Mesopotamia and Persia, of which a relic remains in the Syrian Christianity of Kerala. We belong to this evolutionary cycle, coming from a Jewish matrix and growing through contact with different cultures. Today for the first time this Jewish religion is coming into contact with the culture of Asia in the Far East. We are today at a great moment in the growth of Christianity.

There is no doubt a special quality in a word like *Maranatha,* which attunes us to the earliest tradition of Christianity and takes us back to the roots of our religion. But the name of Jesus, whether in Greek as in the New Testament or in any modern language, has something of the same power. Strange though it may seem at first, the name Jesus itself is a translation from the Hebrew or Aramaic 'Joshua Meshia', so again we see a Greco-Roman transmission at work. We must remember that sounds vibrate through the whole body and have a profound effect on the psyche. It is impossible to conceive the effects of the sounds of a modern city with its endless distractions on the psyche. We are bombarded daily and hourly with these sounds and the images of television. Our times of silence are therefore so important to enable us to let go of all these distractions.

It is the function of the mantra to recollect the soul, to bring it back to its centre and unite the whole person — body, soul and spirit — with the Spirit of God. It is important to remember that prayer and meditation occupy the whole person. We have the body, the physical organism which unites us with all the physical organisms of the universe. We have the soul, the psyche which is the psychological organism with senses, feelings, imagination, reason and will. The centre of the psyche is the ego, that which in Sanskrit is called the *ahamkara,* the 'I-maker'. The psyche is very limited, but beyond it is the spirit, the *Atman* which is the point of self-transcendence. At that point body and soul go beyond their human limitations and open to the infinite, the eternal, the divine. Meditation is passing beyond your body and soul into that point of the spirit.

So meditation is a process of unifying all the faculties of the soul at the point of the spirit where they are penetrated by the light of the truth. At this point all the energies of soul and body are focused. This includes the sexual energy, which we tend to leave out of our spirituality but which is part of our nature. It cannot be eliminated. Either it is expressed in the normal way or it has to be transformed. The sexual energy can be turned towards God in prayer and become a highly positive force. In the *kundalini* method of yoga this energy is transformed into a spiritual force.

Christians should know about this *kundalini* way of yoga. It describes seven centres of psychic energy between the base of the spine and the crown of the head which link us with all the forces of nature and creation. At the *muladhara,* the root chakra, we are in touch with all the physical forces of nature. All the electric, magnetic forces around us vibrate at the base of the spine and this base-energy is called *shakti,* which is the physical energy in nature. Sex is the energy of love in our nature. It is an animal energy originally, but in the human being it goes beyond the animal. So you have to let that energy flow into the *svadisthana* chakra but it must not stop there. For many people it does stop there, and if the energy is stopped at any of these centres it becomes destructive. Unless the sexual energy is present in our prayer we are losing something. If we suppress it, then it either becomes neutral or terribly destructive. There is a very great danger here which many Christians do not realize. They think they must get rid of all their sexual feelings rather than recognizing sex as part of their nature and a gift of God. These feelings have to be surrendered with all the energies of the body and soul, surrendered not suppressed. So the sex energy flows through the sex chakra to the *manipura* or *hara,* the emotional centre. Most people, especially women, live from the *hara,* the emotions, and this is how we relate to other people, either in love, compassion and understanding or in violence and hatred. Then there is the heart chakra, *anahata,* which is the normal centre of the person where the higher and lower chakras are united. St Teresa used to meditate on Jesus in the heart. The devotion to the Sacred Heart is a very beautiful expression of this way. The *visuddha,* or throat chakra, is the source of music, song and poetry as of all speech and words. As the energy rises it becomes more and more human and develops from its animal or vegetative form. Then it passes to the *ajna* chakra which is the mental centre where the mind is focused. In our Christian tradition the lower chakras tend to be suppressed and this leads to an imbalance in the psyche. We live too much in the mind. The energy has to flow through the lower chakras and to be directed by the mind to the higher level of the spirit. But these forces are very powerful so that we need to be watchful. The Buddhists always stress watchfulness for this reason.

So *shakti* rises and eventually reaches the *sahasrara* chakra, the 'thousand-petalled lotus' at the crown of the head. This is where we open up to the whole universe and the transcendent mystery beyond. The energy of life flows from the base of matter through all these stages right up to the transcendent. You can let the energy level flow by visualizing it in your mind. I like to see it flowing from above, with the Holy Spirit descending through all the faculties, right down through the whole of the body and then rising up again and returning to God.

However, blocks tend to occur at each stage. We can find out where the psyche is blocked, and through contemplation we can unify all the faculties of the soul at the point of the Spirit where they are penetrated by the light of truth. This light is essentially a light of love. It is the love of the Holy Spirit poured into the heart which brings us face to face with God. In the Oriental tradition all methods of meditation are ways of coming to that inner centre. But what happens there depends upon your particular faith and tradition. For the Christian the point of the spirit is the point where the love of God is poured into the heart through the Holy Spirit.[3]

What this indicates is that we pray with the body and the soul as well as with the spirit. This is obvious in the Divine Office and the Mass. Bowing and prostrating have an important place in all prayer. In the Hesychast tradition of the Orthodox Church frequent prostrations are an essential part of the prayer; and in the Syrian Church in India, to which I once belonged, there were regular prostrations at every prayer. We used to do forty prostrations one after the other every day during Lent, for example. When we pronounce words and even more when we chant and sing, we are using our bodies in praise. In strictly contemplative prayer the action of the body is reduced to a minimum, but even then there is the movement of the breath. All the Eastern traditions place great emphasis on the breath. Zen meditation, for example, focuses on breathing in and breathing out. Some kind of focus is necessary and we should not forget how we pray with the body. The Indian tradition of the bodily centres or chakras also point to this truth of prayer. Father John paid little attention to the breath, except by insisting that 'one should not stop breathing'. Father Laurence tells me that he did take breath into consideration although he does not talk much about it in his writings. For many people the attuning of the mantra to the breathing is of great importance and helps to bring the body into the heart of the prayer. Personally, I always bring the breath consciously down from the head, the mouth, through the heart and the lower chakras to the soles of the feet. I will always remember a Jungian analyst I knew at Oxford telling me with great conviction, 'One thing I know for certain, women receive the Holy Spirit through the soles of their feet'! Of course, in strict meditation the body is brought as far as possible to stillness so as not to distract the mind. Some insist on an upright position and complete stillness, but I think that a good deal of liberty should be allowed. A technique must never be allowed to take control and hinder the free movement of the Spirit. I have to confess that I meditate best lying down or slightly inclined. Relaxation is so important and our greatest danger is tension. We are all in tension, and even just sitting upright can be a source of tension. We must learn these things as we go and must not be bound by any technique, even a yoga technique.

This applies also to the repetition of the mantra. Father John insisted rather strongly on sticking to the mantra from the beginning to the end, and for many people this may be the best way. Father Laurence has explained to me that Father John's advice was to stay with the mantra for as long as you can say it. If it stops naturally, that is fine, but do not aim to stop saying it. There can be different views on this. For some, as meditation deepens, the mantra may cease or, as they say, go into the heart. This is rather the practice in centering prayer.

The aim must steadily be kept in mind of centering the body and soul in the depth of the spirit, where the human spirit meets the Spirit of God. As St Paul says, 'The Spirit of God bears witness with our spirit that we are children of God.'[4] The spirit is what St Francis de Sales called the 'fine point of the soul'. It is the point of self-transcendence where we go beyond ourselves and receive the divine Spirit into our hearts, that is, into the centre of our being. This is also a meeting point between our spirit and the Spirit of God, and meditation should be that meeting point where the human spirit touches and opens itself to the Holy Spirit. It is interesting how in the New Testament the word 'spirit' is sometimes used for the human and sometimes for the divine — because it is the meeting point. The repetition of the mantra is simply a way of keeping all the faculties of the soul and body centred in this point of the spirit.

This raises the problem of distractions. When we begin to meditate, the mind begins to wander. For most people the activity of the mind never ceases. It has been compared to a monkey in a cage. For people today particularly, and especially for those in the West whose lives are so full of distractions and for whom television with its constant stream of images is a constant source of distraction, the problem of controlling the mind is very acute. We are thinking, thinking, thinking all the time. This is where many Indians find meditation much easier because they do not think so much. They live far more from their bodies, instincts and feelings and can more easily enter the state of meditation. It seems that most people cannot stop the continual flow of thoughts, but what they can do is not to attend to it, to let it flow and quietly observe it like clouds in the sky, while the deeper mind, the spirit within, remains quietly resting in the presence of God. To struggle against distractions can do more harm than good. The great need in meditation is relaxation. Body and mind have to be totally relaxed, so that the spirit can be totally open and receptive to the Spirit of God.

However, there are other forms of distractions which cannot be so easily dismissed. We can let go of ordinary distractions but there are some which are more serious. These are forces in the unconscious which have been repressed and can form a permanent block to the soul if they are not faced. When Father Antony De Mello started an institute for spirituality outside Poona he found that most people, and particularly priests and nuns, had so many psychological blocks that he had to give a course on psychology before he could get on to spirituality. Father John no doubt felt that these forces should be faced at other times and in other ways, and this may be necessary. But I think there are times when they have to be allowed to come up into consciousness in meditation. Many people experience strong feelings of anger, hatred, resentment, fear, anxiety, which are a constant source of disturbance. If they are allowed to come up in meditation they can be opened to a deeper level of consciousness, the consciousness of Christ within.

We realize today that these repressed feelings, which can be such serious blocks in our mind, go right back into infancy. Even before birth the child is subject to the emotional stress of the mother, and we are conditioned in the womb with fears and anxieties. During the first two years after birth the child is much affected by the strains and stresses around it, particularly if there is a difficult marriage or the mother has a disturbed psyche. Then, often when you are forty or fifty you begin to discover what happened to you when you were one year old. These are all repressed feelings, because the child cannot express its feelings. A major example of this, of course, is when a child is neglected or abandoned. This an be an appalling experience. Your mother is your one support, your one source of meaning in life and if she neglects you it can lead to a feeling of being totally lost and totally insecure. Some people have a deep hatred of their mother of father. They do not like to admit their resentment but this feeling, arising from neglect, maltreatment, even sexual abuse, comes out in time. Today we are recognizing the terrible things that children suffer. These are all wounds in our psyche and they continue to afflict us, unless we become aware of their source. Without awareness they cannot be healed, but the moment we become aware and accept them and understand, they can be healed.

This is called the healing of memories. Once they come up you may have to have a psychotherapist to help you. There are various methods. Transactional analysis is one very helpful method; Jungian analysis is another. I had a great friend, who was a doctor and who always had a great problem with losing her temper, which is a common enough problem. When she had gone through analysis she discovered that when her mother died, when she was six, a deep feeling of insecurity had taken root in her. It was from this feeling that her short temper began but knowing this did not cure her. She had more analysis and discovered that at the age of two she had realized she was not wanted because her parents had hoped for a boy. Whenever a child realizes it is not wanted, the feeling of rejection inflicts a terrible wound on the psyche. These wounds must be faced and can be healed. Sometimes these wounds are the very things that awaken you to deeper life because the grace of God comes through the wounds of the psyche. Events can upset you and seem terrifying, while actually it is God opening you up to a deeper level of consciousness.

In meditation these wounds are opened up to the deeper level of consciousness which is Christ within. It is opened with the mantra, and as we go on repeating the mantra we let Christ come in to heal the wounds. This is a way of realizing the compassion of Christ. When he 'descended into hell' he had to face all these hostile forces in the unconscious, and by his patient endurance he was able to set us free. The 'descent into hell' means precisely the descent into the unconscious, and in every human being beneath the personal unconscious with all its childhood wounds is the collective unconscious. Here we all have roots in the origins of humanity.

Some Jungian psychologists think that every human being recapitulates in the womb all the stages of both physical and psychological evolution. If we go deep enough, the whole of humanity's past is within us. There we discover how we are linked with the most primitive tribal people. This is why our rejection of tribal people, in America and Australia for example, is such a disaster. With our conscious mind we reject something deep in ourselves, and until we stop refusing to recognise this, it will never be healed. We have to encounter these deep feelings of the unconscious as Jesus on the cross went into the unconscious and knew the whole of humanity's past. All humanity is in him: he knows the wounds of humanity. He 'bore our wounds on the cross'. This is the source of his compassion. There is nothing that can happen to any child anywhere that Jesus does not know in himself, in the depth of his being, through his experience of our human tragedy. He encounters these forces and overcomes them by endurance. We do not overcome these forces by fighting them and pushing them down by the force of our ego, but rather by letting them come up and surrendering them to God. Then they can be healed and reconciled.

The demons which Jesus encountered and cast out in the New Testament are repressed forces of the unconscious. From childhood on, we repress our anger, fear, hatred and desire, and later these surface in violent ways which we cannot control. We are all faced with it, and Jesus faced this conflict in the human unconscious. By love he totally surrendered to all those contrary forces and allowed them to work on him, and then he carried them in his own body and being to the Father, the source of grace and compassion. That is our redemption.

In this way meditation becomes an encounter with the redeeming Christ. We all need this redemption. Often today we try merely to make the best of life and persuade ourselves that things are not really so bad. But this does not work, and after a time we have to face the deep wounds in ourselves and our whole society and allow the grace of healing to come. The Christ we encounter in meditation is, of course, the risen Christ, who has carried the wounds of our humanity into the bosom of the Father, that is, the ground of being, and brought final reconciliation.

Redemption means that Jesus has taken all the wounds of humanity into himself and surrendered them to God, to the Father. The forces of the unconscious, however, are cosmic forces because humanity is not composed merely of isolated individuals. We all belong to a humanity which is part of the larger cosmos. The forces of the unconscious, of violence, hatred or fear, are, therefore, not only human. This is what is meant by the demonic. There are demons and angels in the unconscious: angels are powers of light, grace and healing while demons are powers of death and destruction, cruelty, revenge and hate. All that is happening among the Israelis and Palestinians, Hindus and Moslems in India, Catholics and Protestants in Northern Ireland is due to collective forces of the unconscious. These people are not responsible to the degree that they are driven by these terrible forces. Hitler was a supreme example of this; he was a psychic. We all have certain psychic experiences, but he was dominated by these destructive forces of the unconscious. I remember speaking to a Jew who came to our monastery during the war who had heard Hitler speak. After three hours of his passionate ranting, with its flood of oratory, he said, you could hardly resist wanting to get up and fight for him.

The forces in the unconscious can be terribly destructive, but they can also be creative. We must never forget the evil forces but we must always remember that all our destructive forces are potentially creative. There is always something good in them, and if you can discover the hidden good, you can release the evil from them and they become creative. One should not want to destroy sin, therefore. Sin always has something good in it. If we can release the good, then the evil with which we started will depart. We do not overcome darkness by fighting it but simply by bringing it into the light. Jesus has taken all our wounds and darkness to the Father and so brought about our final reconciliation. Meditation must always be an encounter with the risen Lord who has reconciled us to the Father in the Spirit. The redeeming Christ loves and understands us, shares our feelings and has complete compassion for us. We don't, of course, have to think of all this when we are meditating; but total surrender in love involves immersion in the depths of the Spirit, who is love, who brings back this reconciliation in Christ and takes us back to the Father, the Source.

To enter deeply into meditation is to enter into the mystery of suffering love. It is to encounter the woundedness of our human nature. We are all deeply wounded from our infancy and bear these wounds in the unconscious. The repetition of the mantra is a way of opening these depths of the unconscious and exposing them to the light. It is first of all to accept our woundedness and thus to realize that this part of the wound of humanity which has grown in us from the beginning of time. All the weaknesses we find in ourselves, and all the things that upset us, we tend to try to push aside and get rid of. But we cannot do this. We have to accept that 'this is me' and allow grace to come and heal it all. That is the great secret of suffering, not to try to push it back but to open the depths of the unconscious and realize that we are not isolated individuals when we meditate but are entering into the whole inheritance of suffering in the human family.

The demons or devils encountered in the New Testament are then the repressed forces of the unconscious which torment human-ity. But the unconscious also contains the redemptive forces, the healing powers that can set us free. Once the active mind has been silenced, because it is the active mind that keeps all this repressed, we can encounter the deeper mind which is exposed to good and evil forces, to angels and demons. Meditation, as the Fathers of the Desert and St Benedict so clearly realized, is an encounter with these contrary forces. They often said that they went to the desert to 'fight with demons', because they knew all these forces would come out from the unconscious. People often think that if they get away from their external activities then everything will be all right, but then they discover these strong feelings beginning to surface. That is why meditation is dangerous. To silence the rational, discursive mind is to expose oneself to these conflicting powers. This is of course also the danger of taking psychedelic drugs, which open up the unconscious. They stop the rational mind and open the unconscious, and sometimes wonderful, creative powers emerge in ecstasy. But at the same time, the opposite powers begin to come up. It is dangerous precisely because the person taking drugs is exposed to both the creative and destructive forces.

As Christians, we have to open ourselves to the power of the Holy Spirit which, through the mantra, keeps us in touch with the redeeming Christ, the power which alone can reconcile those opposing forces within us. This shows the necessity for meditation to be supported by *lectio divina*. We need this support all the time because if we expose ourselves to these inner forces without support we can be torn to pieces. But when we rely on the mantra to keep us in touch with Christ in the Holy Spirit then we have something which gives us control and sets us free from that destructive power. Unless we meditate on the Scriptures and learn to understand the mystery of redemption, we cannot encounter these hidden forces without injury. Many young people today rush into meditation and then encounter these powers without warning. We have seen people like this at our ashram, and they become quite unhinged.

In the Middle Ages there were four stages recognized in the course of prayer: *lectio, meditatio, oratio, contemplatio*. We begin with *lectio*, reading, which is the normal way of initiation into a spiritual tradition today. We then pass to *meditatio*, which is reflecting on the meaning of the Scriptures you have read, applying it to your own life and realizing how the divine mystery revealed in the Scriptures is present and active in your own life. We then pass to *oratio*, turning to God in praise, thanksgiving, worship and prayer and intercession for our own needs and the needs of the world. Finally, this leads us to *contemplatio*, the recollection of the divine mystery in the heart, the inner centre of our being where we come directly under the power of the Holy Spirit. These are the normal stages of prayer and we need to keep in touch with them. We should not let the mantra take us out of normal Christian prayer. But *lectio, meditatio* and *oratio* should normally lead to *contemplatio* as the fullness of Christian prayer.

As the great Dominican theologian Father Garrigou-Lagrange showed us years ago, contemplation is a fulfilment of baptism. All the gifts of the Spirit given in baptism flower in contemplation which is thus a normal fulfilment of Christian life. This is still how we need to see it, leading to the recollection of the divine mystery in the heart where we come directly under the power of the Holy Spirit. The Holy Spirit is everywhere, but our direct contact is at the point of the spirit. Otherwise it is mediated through people and the experience of God can be distorted. Redemptive power is to be found at the point of direct communion with the Holy Spirit, and there it comes into our whole being and can transform us.

There is a danger of thinking of the mantra as a kind of magic, so that we have only to go on repeating it and we will get whatever we are seeking. This would be delusion and the mantra would then become a technique and so virtually self-defeating. The mantra must always be an expression of faith and love. That is why I like a mantra which has some relation to Christian experience, as *Maranatha* obviously has. The Jesus Prayer is an even more obvious example. This link of faith is very important. Many mantras, as in Transcendental Meditation, are merely psychological, attuning your psyche in some way, but this does not go far enough. A Christian mantra which opens you up in faith and love to the presence of Christ within is very important. Father John possessed this foundation of deep faith. He was a man of deep knowledge and wisdom. You can see in all his writings how deeply immersed he was in the knowledge of the Christian mystery. We too must bring that into our meditation. Contemplation, properly speaking, can only come through faith and love. The mantra is a means of allowing faith and love to be activated.

Love brings us face to face with God. It also exposes us to the deep wounds in our nature and compels us to face the suffering of humanity from the beginning of time. Love is terrible in the way it makes us face our own wounds and the sufferings of others. But it breeds compassion. This is the wonder of Mahayana Buddhism. Early Buddhism was focused more upon passing beyond the suffering of the world and entering nirvana, inner peace and silence. But the Mahayana realized that when you enter that depth you discover the compassion of the Buddha. The Dalai Lama today expresses this wonderful compassion, not only for human beings but for all sentient beings, the whole creation.

Love brings us into the presence of Christ who bears in himself humanity's wounds. Meditation, therefore, far from shutting us up in ourselves, opens us — as Father John put it — to an 'infinite expansion of spirit'. Our compassion extends to the whole of suffering humanity, which is both revealed and healed by the suffering of Christ on the cross. On the one hand the suffering of Christ tells of humiliation, cruelty, death and destruction. On the other hand at the same time, it is the revelation of total love and healing. The cross is healing. Crucifixes may, however, fail to express the whole meaning of the cross. In the later Middle Ages crucifixes emphasized the sufferings of Christ so strongly that they obscured the love of Christ. It was not until about the sixth century that the crucifix became common at all. Byzantine churches always place the figure of Christ in glory in the apse, suggesting that we go through the cross to the glorified Christ with the angels and saints. Syrian churches have the 'cross of light' which similarly emphasizes Christ as reigning from the cross. With St Francis of Assisi and the medieval focus on suffering, these aspects of the cross were overshadowed. But the suffering Christ, the glorified Christ and the cosmic Christ are all aspects of the same reality which we have to keep in mind.

Father John insisted that our meditation must lead us to this contemplation of the Christian mystery in all its depth. This in turn must be expressed by compassion in our lives. In so doing we overcome the duality of the conscious mind which separates us from God and from one another and we realize that this duality has been overcome in Christ. Original sin is a fall into duality. The original human being was created to be unified in body, soul and spirit, and so to be open to God. The fall of humanity is the fall from the spirit into the psyche, which means into the ego, the separated self. Instead of being a movement, a continuous opening toward God in the spirit, we fall into our ego and become shut up in the fear and conflict with others. Once you fall into your psyche you become subject to the dualism of the rational mind. The rational mind based on the experience of the senses is inherently dualistic. It sees everything in terms of opposites, mind and matter, subject and object, truth and error, right and wrong.

But always beyond the dualism of the mind is the unity of the spirit. Meditation takes us beyond the dualities to the unified spirit. Christ came to set us free from this dualism. He is the one who broke through the division in our nature. St Paul says he 'broke down the dividing wall' and reconciled us in one body on the cross. In the Temple in Jerusalem there was a wall which no Gentile could pass on pain of death. This is the wall Jesus broke down, opening up the Temple to all humanity. But we have erected the walls again and divided the world.

We need today to take very seriously the view of humanity as one body, one organic whole. The Fathers had this strong sense of the Adam who is in all humanity. St Thomas Aquinas, in a beautiful phrase, said, 'Omnes homines, unus homo,' 'All men are one man.' We are all members of that one Man who fell and became divided in conflict and confusion. Jesus restored humanity, not only Jews or Christians or any particular group, to that oneness. In the new Adam the human race becomes conscious of its fundamental unity and of its unity with the cosmos. This is what we are recovering today, as we rediscover our common humanity. I think many modern means, like television as it brings events from all around the world so close to us, help us to realize that others' problems are part of our own concerns.

Both types of awareness have come to us today, seeing humanity as a whole and seeing humanity as part of the cosmic whole. We are all part of this planet, united by it and growing and living from it. We are all parts of each other, growing through contact with one another as one organic whole. We are recovering that unity beyond duality. Humanity had to go through dualism, to learn the difference between right and wrong, good and evil, truth and error. It is necessary to go through that stage of separating and dividing, but then you have to transcend it. The Old Testament generally reflects this duality: it was always the Israelites who were to be rejected. The good were to be separate and the evil condemned. This dualism runs all through the Jewish tradition.

Jesus came from that Jewish tradition and often uses its language of rejection and condemnation. Yet all the time he was going beyond it and taking us to the point where we transcend all dualities. This is marvellously expressed in St John's Gospel: 'May they all be one: as you, Father, are in me, and I in you, so also may they be in us.'[5] Here Jesus shows that he is totally one with the Father and yet he is not the Father. It is a non-dual relationship. It is not one and it is not two. When two people unite in love they become one and yet keep their distinctiveness. Jesus and the Father had this total communion in love, and he asks us to become one with him as he is one with the Father: total oneness in the non-dual being of the Godhead. It is the Christian calling, to recover this unity. In India *advaita* has many forms; some are not at all satisfactory, but the idea of *advaita,* non-duality is fundamental to Christian understanding today.

Christianity came out of a tradition of moral dualism. It then passed into the Greco-Roman culture which was based on a metaphysical dualism. But today it is meeting the religion of Asia, and we are beginning to discover the principle of non-duality. The rational mind demands that everything be one or two, while non-duality, which is beyond the rational, affirms a relationship which is not one and not two. It is only through meditation that we get beyond this duality. We are being called to recover unity beyond duality as our birthright, and it is this alone which can answer the deepest needs of the world today.

I am planning a book of readings in the Scriptures of the world in which I try to show that every religion — Hinduism, Buddhism, Taoism, Islam, Judaism and Christianity — has a dualistic element as its starting point but then moves into this non-dualism. Judaism and Islam are particularly dualistic and can be full of terrible denunciations of unbelievers and descriptions of their doom and punishment. This is a stage in religion which has to be transcended and people must learn to go beyond that stage. The Sufis of the eighth and ninth centuries in Islam went right beyond it into non-dualism, like the Jews in the Kabbala and Meister Eckhart in our Christian tradition. Every religion goes beyond dualism through its mystical tradition.

This is our calling and our hope. Meditation is the only way to go beyond dualism. As long as you think rationally you will have a dualistic attitude. But when you stop the mind, you discover the unifying principle behind everything. I think that in the meditation movement God is leading humanity through this dualism. It is a call that has gone all over the world. Everywhere people are meeting together, discovering this need and responding to it in the different ways of meditation. We are all being called to open our hearts to the non-dual mystery which is the mystery of love revealed in the Trinity.

In the doctrine of the Trinity the ultimate Reality is seen as Being in relationship or Being in love. The ultimate Reality is not a solitary person nor an impersonal Absolute. It is a communion of persons in love. Every being seeks to express and communicate itself. In the human being the body is one means by which we

56

express ourselves and communicate with others. But the highest expression of our being is the mind. It is through the mind that we find words to express and communicate ourselves. In the Godhead as conceived in the Christian tradition, the Word of God is the expression of the mind of God. It is the self-manifestation of the eternal Wisdom; and the Spirit of God, the Holy Spirit, is the self-communication of the eternal Being, infinite love, which is manifested in the whole of creation and comes to a head in the person of Jesus Christ. It is to the experience of this eternal Wisdom communicated in the love of the Holy Spirit that our meditation should lead us.

1 Basil Pennington, *Centering Prayer,* Doubleday 1982.
2 1 Corinthians 16:22.
3 Romans 5:5.
4 Romans 8:16.
5 John 17:21.

4

Mantra Meditation in the Eastern Tradition

In using a mantra as a method of meditation Father John was drawing on the Eastern tradition, though he was careful to show that it had a basis of tradition in the Christian Church as well. In order to understand the full power of the mantra, we need to reflect on this wider context. Meditation with a mantra has now spread all over the world, and we need to compare the Christian method introduced by Father John with other methods based on the Eastern tradition, the sources of which go back beyond recorded history. All ancient religion was based on a sense of the sacred, of a mysterious presence in nature and in the human heart, which could be invoked by words and actions, by chanting and ritual. The chanting invoked the divine presence and the ritual enacted its manifestation in different forms.

From the earliest times we know that human beings have been aware of a mysterious presence, the sacred. All ancient religion had a profound sense of the sacred pervading the whole universe. In India it is still powerful in the villages, everywhere. It is basic to life. There is an awareness of a presence that awakens in you a word, a song, in response to the rhythm of nature. There is a great rhythm behind the whole universe, and when we chant or sing, we put ourselves in touch, in tune, with this rhythm. Deep music touches the depths of this rhythm. I was in a Benedictine monastery in England for twenty years. Chanting the Gregorian chant every day has a wonderful power. The ancient music puts you immediately in touch with the sacred.

A chant is a typical way of tuning in to the rhythm of the universe, and that is what we all need. Beyond music, there are certain words that open up the mystery of the divine presence. In India, the great word is *Brahman* which comes from the root *brh*, meaning 'to swell' or 'to grow'. Before there were temples, in the ancient Hindu tradition based on the *yajna*, the vedic sacrifice, a fire was built in the courtyard of a house and offerings made. Agni, the god of fire in the heavens above, came down to the earth from the sun, consumed the offering, and brought it back to heaven. This was a way of relating the world to heaven. While the priest was offering the sacrifice, a word rose up within him, swelled up in him, and he would say, *'Brahman, Brahman,'* in response to the great mystery that was in the sacrifice. So the word *Brahman* came to mean 'the power in the sacrifice', which was also seen to be the power in the universe.

To sacrifice is 'to make a thing sacred', and ancient people understood that the universe was based on sacrifice, a turning of things over to God. In traditional Hindu teaching, *Brahman*, the Source of the Universe, came to be used as the name for the Godhead as the power present in the sacrifice and in the whole universe. The word which came to be recognized as the supreme mantra, the word which for the Hindu, above all, invokes the presence of God, was the *pranava*, 'OM' (which can also be spelled AUM). It is supposed to embrace all sounds. It has a tremendous sanctity in India. There is a beautiful text, in the Maitri Upanishad, which says, 'There is an OM which is silent and an OM which is sound; and the sound comes out of the silence.' *Brahman* was seen as the silence and out of that silence comes this word, this OM, and then it returns to him. When we utter the OM, we are invoking the divine presence and surrendering ourselves to it. The OM takes us back to the Source, back to the *Brahman*. How tremendously sacred it is!

Of this word, it is said in the Katha Upanishad, 'I will tell you that Word which all the vedas glorify, all sacrifice expresses, all sacred studies and holy life seek — that Word is OM.' So you see what it means to a Hindu. It is true that many Hindus today are losing their tradition, but there are always people who preserve it. And it is extremely important for all of us that this tradition should be preserved. We recognize the sacredness above all. One of the problems in the modern world, especially in the West, is that we have almost abolished the sacred. Of course, there are reasons for this. At the time of the Reformation and Renaissance, it was felt that sacred ritual was superstitious, it was keeping people away from a wider knowledge, the knowledge of science, and so we left the sacred behind and have entered into a profane world. In the West everything is done in the context of the present, in this time and space. But in India and elsewhere in ancient times, everything was done in relation to the sacred.

I had a beautiful experience when we first came to the ashram. In the little village of Tannirpalli there are a lot of weavers, and we organized a weavers' co-operative society to help them. I used to go to their meetings from time to time. They never began a meeting without invoking the presence of God, and even when the account books were produced, a sacred paste was put on them to sanctify them. Everything has to be made sacred. We have one beautiful rite which we always observe in October when all the instruments used in daily life are assembled and solemnly blessed. Bicycles and typewriters and TV sets, whatever we have, is put out and blessed. I visited a doctor once on that day. All his surgical instruments were laid out and a Brahmin priest came and blessed them. A beautiful idea really. Everything is made sacred. Words like OM and *Brahman* were used in these blessings. A counterpart for Tibetan Buddhists is the phrase, *'OM mani padme hum'* (Oh, the jewel in the heart of the lotus'). That is the jewel in the heart of the universe, the mystery in the heart of everything.

This takes us to the heart of mantric meditation. It is a way of transcending the surface mind and entering into the depths of the soul where the hidden mystery is found. This, of course, is the great need today — to get beyond surface phenomena. Technology has developed to such an extent that we have to make a particular effort to get beyond the sense phenomena, noise and random impressions, and enter into the silence in order to become aware of the sacred mystery. Beyond and behind and within it all is the sacred mystery always. That is what meditation and the mantra are supposed to do for us.

The Upanishads record the most profound search into this hidden mystery in human history. Something happened in India in the fifth and sixth centuries before Christ that broke through outer appearances, beyond the body, soul and mind, into the hidden mystery of the universe. The early Upanishads are a record of it. There are supposed to be 108 Upanishads, but most of them came later, and only ten or twelve of the earliest are really essential. These are the classical Upanishads and they are not difficult. There is an excellent translation by Juan Mascaro[1] that provides in short from the essence of the teaching.

For the Hindu today, the aim is still to see behind the surface of life, behind all human experience and psychology to the hidden mystery at the heart of every person and thing. The ancient Hindus looked within and saw the *Atman,* the Spirit, as the source of consciousness, the ground of being. They looked outside of themselves and saw the hidden mystery of the universe, the *Brahman.* the Great discovery was that *Atman* is *Brahman.* 'The Self is *Brahman.*' The root and ground of consciousness, of being, is one with the root and ground of the whole creation. We are one with the whole creation at the depths of our being. It is such a wonderful intuition!

The *sannyasi* gives up family, house and home, and wanders the earth, living in caves, searching to become one with the supreme mystery, the *Atman,* the Spirit. A great example was Ramana Maharshi whose ashram is about two hundred miles from ours. Though he passed away in 1950, he is still considered the great exemplar of 'a realized soul', one who realized *Brahman.* The story is a wonderful one. When he was seventeen, attending an American school in Madurai, he seemed a normal Brahmin boy until he had an experience that convinced him that he was going to die. He went into his room near the temple (I visited it once) and lay down on the floor and surrendered himself to death. He let his body become stiff, he stopped breathing, and said to himself, 'Now, this body is dead, am I dead?' At that moment he underwent a mystical death. He realized suddenly and totally, 'I am not this body. I am an eternal spirit.' He never lost that sense. He was seventeen at the time and did not die until he was seventy, but never did he forget, 'I am not this body. I am an eternal spirit.' He died of cancer after several operations on his arm, but he regarded that as totally outside his true self. He suffered a lot and groaned at night, but when friends sympathized, he said, 'I am not suffering. My body is suffering. I am not suffering.' It is this profound intuition that is at the source of Hinduism.

To interpret and articulate this intuition remained and remains a problem. How exactly was this *Brahman,* this source of being, related to human consciousness? Between the eighth and eighteenth centuries, many philosophical systems — some not unlike the scholasticism of Christian theology — evolved. Each tried to relate the Supreme God with the human being. And each was different. The most famous school perhaps is that of Shankara, the *advaitic* school of the eighth century, which emphasized the oneness of God and the world. God and the soul, are 'not two'. Shankara did not say that God and the soul are the same, but that they are not two; they exist in a transcendental relationship. Among educated Hindus, this is still the most common philosophy.

Then came Ramanuja, a philosopher of the eleventh century, who taught *Vishistadvaita* or a qualified non-dualism. According to Shankara, there is not duality at all and, therefore, the personal God rather fades away. But Ramanuja was a devotee of a personal God. He placed the personal God above all, but still saw that everything was one with God.

Then came Madhva with a third system which favours duality *(dvaita)* and teaches that God is different from the world and the soul. Most Christians would agree with this, but it has never caught on in India. Hindus tend to accept either *Advaita* or *Vishistadvaita*. Incidentally, St Thomas Aquinas always insisted that the world is a relationship to God. The world does not exist alongside God, the world 'here' and God 'there'. The world is a relationship *to* God. It exists *from* God and *to* God. It has no being in itself at all. Thus, we are very near to a kind of *advaita* in our basic Christian teaching.

Another doctrine which may be of interest is called *bhedabheda*. *Bheda* is 'difference'; *abheda is* 'non-difference'. The teachers of this doctrine said the relationship between God and the world is both different and non-different. They left it as a paradox. Interestingly in our time Prabhupada brought this teaching to America with the Hari Krishna movement. Throughout its history, Hinduism has struggled with the mystery of the relation between God and the soul, God and the world.

It is fascinating to study philosophical systems and their historical development, yet we must remember that they are attempting to express in logical terms a mystery that cannot be properly expressed in words. That is the problem. It is beyond words, beyond thought. That is why all philosophy must eventually take refuge in the mantra, to go beyond thought and seek the answer in meditation. When we meditate we let the senses become calm and quiet, and we let the mind become calm and quiet, until we are no longer speaking and no longer thinking. Then awareness can come, the awareness of the inner mystery.

Insofar as we are thinking and verbal beings, however, the question, of course, never completely goes away. We still want at least to approach an answer: How can we express this mystery in terms that correspond to our deepest intuition and make it intelligible to rational understanding? This is at the heart of the Christian-Hindu dialogue today: How do we understand the relation between

God and soul, God and world? There are very subtle differences, and so this is a real theological task.

While the Hindu approaches the mystery from the point of view of inner experience, recognizing the immanent presence of God in the human soul and the world, the Hebrew revelation came in the form of the manifestation of a transcendent God. The God of Israel is separate from the world and humanity. He rules from above. He creates the world, he creates human beings. He may descend, he may speak, but he remains transcendent. The word that describes the God of Israel is 'holy', which means 'separate'. God is holy because he is separate from the world. A human being is holy when he or she is separated from the world. When you go into religion, dedicate your life, become a holy person, you are separated from the world. A gift offered in sacrifice is holy because it is separated from profane use. While Hinduism is non-dualistic, the religion of Israel is based on a profound dualism that extends to every level of being. Human beings are separate from the world in which they live; Israel is a holy nation separate from all other nations of the world; the good are separated from the evil and have a different destiny. All of this stems from the profound experience of Israel, from Moses and the prophets, of a transcendent God.

This insistence on the transcendence of God is a problem today. God can become so sacred and so far beyond that we lose touch with him. That is why Jesus brought it all down to earth by speaking of God as *Abba,* Father, insisting on an intimate relationship between himself and the Father. The God of Islam is even further away than the God of Israel. The Allah of the Koran is totally transcendent. Islam means 'surrender'. You surrender to God. The relation of the Muslim to God is that of slave, *abd* — a slave of God. A Muslim's duty is obedience. Jesus said, 'I will not call you servants. I call you friends.'[2] He made love the basis. That is a further stage of religion. The transcendent God of Jewish tradition chose Israel from among all the nations of the world to proclaim his message and to be a light to other nations. Jesus came to fulfil this call of Israel, but he opened it to the whole world in a totally new, personal and non-exclusive way.

Again and again in the Old Testament, God says, 'I am the first and the last. Beside me there is no God. Who is like me?' There is an absolute difference between the God of Israel and all other gods. According to Islamic tradition, Allah too is alone among gods, and the Koran is the one, supreme revelation. It is difficult to go beyond this, and that is a problem. How can we reconcile the Muslim and Hebraic claim of absolute transcendence with the Hindu and Buddhist experience of an immanent presence of the sacred in the depths of the human soul and in the universe? The difference has too often led people to violence. Though Gandhi did a wonderful thing in leading India toward independence, as soon as he was gone, the strife was terrible between Hindus and Muslims. Thousands were massacred in the name of religion. That is one reason that people become atheists. They say, 'These religions make people kill one another. Let's get away from them all.' Of course, that is not the answer. We have to find the real answer.

Can we, in meditation, reach a point where opposite ideals are reconciled? As long as we remain on the level of conceptual thought, there is no resolution to the distinction between the transcendent and the immanent. But when we enter into meditation and go to the source, the secret place of the heart, an answer can be found. We are pilgrims, seeking to find in our own self, in our own heart, the reconciliation of opposites. One of the most profound of contemporary insights is the felt need for reconciliation. We tend to think in dualistic terms that opposites — black and white, good and evil, truth and error — cannot be reconciled. But the deeper intuition is that behind all opposites there is a movement of inter-relationship, as in the doctrine of Taoism, the Chinese theory of *yin* and *yang*. The *Tao Te Ching,* the greatest Chinese classic, presents a wonderful view of the unity of all things in their opposites.

A version of this view can be found in the Christian tradition as well. Nicholas of Cusa, an eminent Roman cardinal of the fifteenth century, wrote a splendid book called *The Vision of God* in which he speaks of *'conincidentia oppositorum'*, the 'coincidence of opposites'. There is a point where opposites coincide. Our dualistic mind always sees them as different, but when we get deep enough, we realize that reconciliation is possible. I think that Jesus came to reconcile opposites. 'God was in Christ, reconciling the world to himself'. This is our task: in meditation, to reconcile transcendence and immanence.

The Hindu and the Buddhist in their meditation go beyond all outer appearances and experience the inner reality of the Self, the Spirit, which is beyond all name and form. Buddhists will not speak of God or even of the soul. Thus some people say that since Buddhists do not believe in God or the soul, they cannot have any religion at all. But it is simply a difference of outlook, of language, of concept. Behind the denial of a personal God and an individual soul, is a profound intuitive grasp of the hidden mystery behind God, behind the world. The Buddha did not want to name it. He did not actually deny God, but he would not name it and simply called it *'nirvana'*, which means 'blowing out', the extinction of all dualities. When you get beyond opposition, you find bliss. Out of the negations of the Buddha — that all is suffering, all is passing, all is unreal — comes a profound sense of joy. If you read the *Dharmapada,* the great classic of early Buddhism, you will find that it says again and again, 'In joy we live.' This is the joy that comes when you get beyond conflict and realize the mysterious unity of being.

That the Buddhist has a profound religion, there is no doubt. But it is not our way of putting things. Theirs is a concept of absolute oneness: God, the soul, and the universe are experienced as a total unity in which no differences appear. This has been the experience of countless saints and sages from the earliest times to the present. To many people today it has come as a profound revelation of the ultimate meaning of life. Whether through yoga or Zen or *vipassana,* this enlightenment is seen as a final revelation of absolute truth. Innumerable people have rejected Christianity, a personal God, dualism, good and evil, and feel that in Buddhism they find the answer to all their problems. They find enlightenment. It is not the final truth, but they find something and we have to recognize its value. We cannot just dismiss what is clearly a profound experience.

A Christian cannot ignore the testimony of traditions that go back over two thousand years and have shown themselves capable of transforming the lives of people all over the world. Christian meditation with a mantra is also a way of entering into the depth of the soul and discovering the presence of the hidden mystery within. But how does a Christian understand this mystery? This is what we have to discern. What is the difference between the Hindu, the Buddhist, the Muslim, and the Christian experience? All alike enter into the depth and go beyond the body and senses, mind and concepts, and are awakened to the mystery within. Each one experiences and expresses it in a somewhat different way. How do we reconcile these differences? To answer this, we need to try to discern what is the particular Christian experience of the mystery.

How does a Christian understand the mystery? It is, first of all, a discovery of the Spirit within, the Spirit of which St Paul says, 'These things God has revealed to us through his Spirit, for the Spirit searches everything, even the depths of God.'[3] In each human being there is the Spirit that 'searches everything, even the depths of God'. This, for the Christian, is the hidden mystery.

Clearly, all Christians meet with Hindus, Buddhists, and Muslims in the depth of the Spirit beyond reason, which is known in meditation as we open our hearts to what St Paul calls the 'mystery of Christ'. Again and again, in the New Testament, especially in Ephesians and Colossians, one finds references to *'mysterium Christi'*. In speaking of mystery, Paul uses a word which was current in the world of his day because of the Greek 'mystery' religions. All over the Roman Empire at the time of the early Church, there were 'mystery' religions in which, through various rituals and teaching, people tried to make contact with the hidden mystery of the universe, behind the universe, behind their own lives. Of course, they varied greatly in character, but some of them were very deep, and the Church drew on them in many ways.

The possibility of a Spirit beyond the rational mind can be a problem, since for some people the rational mind is the mind. There is nothing beyond it. If you try to go beyond it, you are a lunatic, If you tell some people that, beyond the rational mind and all its concepts and dualities, there is true wisdom, they think that you are mad. But that is what we call the 'mystery' and is what St Paul proclaimed as the wisdom and mystery of Christ.[4] We have to say that there is something beyond science and philosophy and any form of rational knowledge. For a Christian, this is precisely the mystery of Christ.

The object of Christian meditation is to encounter Christ in the depths of one's being, not mediated by words and thoughts, but known by his presence in the Spirit. When Jesus was about to leave his disciples, he promised to send them the 'Spirit of Truth' to guide them to all truth. It is this Spirit that we encounter when we enter into the depths of our own spirit. As St Paul says, 'The Spirit of God bears witness with our spirit that we are children of God.'[5] So in meditation we are entering into that depth of the spirit where we encounter the Spirit of God.

Of course, we have to read the Bible. We need words and thoughts. We cannot simply go into the spirit without the help of words, because the mind needs the instruction of faith. We must begin by meditating on Scripture and the teachings of the Church, but we also have to go beyond them. And that upsets people who think the Bible is everything and that one must stay with the Bible alone. But the Bible is still words and thoughts, whereas the Word of God is beyond words and thoughts. It is a hidden mystery. Jesus himself is beyond the Bible. He, not the Bible, is the ultimate Reality.

Jesus did not leave us the New Testament. That came later. He left us the Holy Spirit. That was his own spirit, the Spirit of the Father. In meditation, we try to go beyond the limitation of words and thoughts to open our hearts to the hidden mystery of the Spirit and to be really in the presence of Christ and the Father, to enter into the mystery of the Trinity. This is a tremendous undertaking. We are trying to break through to the ultimate truth of reality. As long as you are in the world of dualities, of churches and doctrines and rituals, there are always conflicts and always will be. It is only when we go beyond all outer expressions, all sacraments (outward signs) and enter into the hidden mystery that we can touch the point that unites us all.

As long as we are in the way of ritual and doctrine, we are all fighting one another. But when we get beyond ritual and doctrine, which are signs (and necessary in their own way) to the mystery itself, then we touch the point of human unity where religions can be reconciled. We are here to reconcile religious conflicts in the world. It is a terrible responsibility. This is our calling: to enter into that depth of the Spirit where we encounter Jesus' own Spirit. Jesus lives in the Church through his Spirit. When he departed from his disciples, he ascended and returned in the Spirit to dwell in every disciple, in every human being, because no one is outside his grace. There is a presence within us. When we enter into the silence of meditation, we encounter the real presence of Christ.

One must be careful in speaking of the 'real presence' of Christ in the Eucharist. Of course, this is central in our life and religion, but it is a sacramental presence. In the Eucharist Jesus is present under the sign of bread and wine. We need signs to touch and taste and share, but the Presence itself is not limited by the sign. Jesus is present in the heart. When we leave church, we do not leave Jesus in the tabernacle. The bread is a sign of his presence, but we carry him along in our hearts. In meditation, we try to go directly to the presence in the heart. That is our aim.

In the depth of the Spirit we discover the depths of our own spirit, and this is where immanence and transcendence come together. We all need to reflect on it, because the Spirit is both immanent and transcendent. The Spirit is that point where we go beyond our ego, beyond the limited self, and open on the divine, and meet the transcendent God. At that intersection of the Spirit God and the soul, the transcendent and immanent meet. Some may emphasize the immanence and almost forget about the transcendence; some may emphasize the transcendence and pay little attention to the immanence. But we need to recognize that the more deeply we go into ourselves and find God within, the more we realize his transcendence.

I think that love is the key. In love, there are two, and each has to go beyond the other. They have to transcend their differences and meet at a point where they become one. In the inner mystery of the soul, we have to become aware of the indwelling presence of the Spirit and then surrender ourselves to the Spirit of God within. It is a dual movement. Sometimes we can emphasize our oneness in the Spirit, and just meditate on the presence of God. At other times, we need to reflect on the infinite transcendence of God as we open our hearts, giving thanks and praise. These two movements can go on in our meditation. Never forget the wonderful saying of St. Paul: 'The love of God is poured into our hearts through the Holy Spirit who is given us.'[6] We enter into the 'heart' and find the love of God pouring in 'from above'. The transcendent mystery enters into the depths of our being and becomes an immanent presence there.

The Spirit is at once the depths of our own being, the inner person, in which our whole being finds its centre, and also the point where we are entirely open to God, the infinite, eternal Spirit. As St Paul says, 'Anyone united to the Lord becomes one spirit with him.'[7] Here we have the meeting of the Jewish sense of God's infinite transcendence with the Eastern sense of his immanent presence. Is it to be wondered at that this is difficult to express in words? There is a wonderful verse by Manikka Vasakar, a great Tamil mystic, that says, 'You are all that is. You are nothing that is.' The first part sounds like pantheism, but it is turned into a paradox. God is in everything. He totally pervades the universe, yet, at the same time, he totally transcends the universe which is nothing in comparison with him.

When we go deeply into prayer, God is in us and we are in him. It is to this depth of non-duality that Jesus leads us in the gospel of John when he prays for his disciples: 'As you, Father, are in me and I in you, may they also be in us...I in them and you in me, that they may be completely one.'[8] That is the summit of the Christian religion.

It is now generally accepted that there were three periods in the formation of the New Testament. The first was the thirty-three years when Jesus was living as a Jew in Palestine, first with his family and then with his disciples, speaking Aramaic. During this time he preached, suffered, was crucified, and rose from the dead. The second period was from about 30 AD to 60 AD, when the story of Jesus and his teaching was handed on through the churches in different versions. The first were in Aramaic, but as they spread through the Greek world they were translated. Then between 60 AD and 90 AD, the gospels as we know them, were written. The evangelists drew on various sources, including an oral tradition that had come down through the early churches. By 60 AD, the original apostles were passing away and the need for a permanent written record was clear. We have to read our gospels critically. They are not simply the words of Jesus, not simply the story of Jesus. The accounts of events have come down through witnesses, through the churches, and through the guidance of the Holy Spirit, but the gospels are different and there are conflicting elements in them that we have to recognize.

St John's gospel was written between 90 AD and the end of the century. It is a profound reflection on the whole mystery of Christ. There is no doubt that the story and the teaching have come through

71

a particular group of churches, but it is also evident that the writer was attempting to interpret his own experience. He draws it out of the depths of the teaching of Jesus. We come nearest to the 'heart' of Christ in the gospel of St John. It is so profound. It was a tremendous grace that the teaching could be transmitted in that way. When Jesus prays that 'they may be one as you are in me and I in you, that they may be one in us', we are being asked to enter into the hidden mystery of the Godhead, to share Jesus' own knowledge of God and love of God; to share in and with and through him in the knowledge of the Father. That is the Christian revelation. It is not God 'up there' and the servant down below. It is the human being, drawn into the hidden mystery of the Godhead, sharing in the love and the knowledge which *is* the Godhead. The Godhead is a communion of knowledge and love. And we are being drawn into it. That is our calling.

That is why meditation is so important. Sacramental rites are wonderful and necessary; the Mass is central. But we are still using external signs: churches, candles, crucifixes, vestments, bread and wine. All these things are external. The mystery is coming *through* these signs. Sometimes the signs can be an embarrassment. There are often so many distractions in a church. But when we get beyond all the outer appearances and enter into the silence, we can encounter the Spirit of God, the Spirit of Jesus, and be in total communion in the heart. That is what we seek: a communion with God, in Christ, which is non-dual. We are no longer two. We are one, but not simply one without any distinction: one in relationship. The Persons of the Trinity are subsistent relationships. Love is a dynamism. It is not a solitary thing. The two commune with each other, penetrate into each other, become one with each other; and that is a non-dual relationship, a mystery we cannot express in words. That is where the gospel is leading us. It is a communion of love where each is in the other and knows no other, in a mystery of self-transcendence since in love the two become united, and one is not lost in the other.

That is the mystery of love. The two become more themselves when fulfilled in love.

This is the ultimate Christian experience of God, and it is to this that our Christian meditation must lead us. That is why I say that I feel God is calling us. We are not doing it of ourselves. God is calling us to this way of meditation, to this experience of God in the hidden mystery of the heart. People are being drawn into this all over the world, some as Hindus, some as Buddhists. Often the Christian mystery is not given to them in a meaningful way. They think Christianity is an external religion for 'ordinary' people, but not sufficient for those who are really searching for God. We have to witness to the fact that there is a Christian mystery that can be experienced in the depth of the soul and answers the deepest need of our human nature. That is the challenge: to witness to this gift in meditation, in contemplative prayer through the mantra. John Main found the way for us all.

1 *Upanishads* (trans. Juan Mascaro), Penguin 1965.
2 John 15:15. It should be noted, however, that in Sufism Islam moves into a religion of pure love.
3 1 Corinthians 2:10.
4 Ephesians 3:4.
5 Romans 8:16.
6 Romans 5:5.
7 1 Corinthians 6:17.
8 John 17:21, 23.

5

The Future of Contemplative Life in the Church

We have been thinking of this whole growth of contemplative prayer, the movement through meditation groups, and how it has introduced a new way of life into the Church and for humanity as a whole. We have seen how Father John Main, by introducing meditation with a mantra, renewed an ancient tradition of contemplative prayer in the Benedictine order and how he then extended it to lay people. We have seen how this tradition of meditation derives from the Fathers of the Desert and was passed on by Cassian to St Benedict and how it has now spread throughout the world. We have also seen how it has roots in ancient India and has become a typical method of prayer in Eastern religions. It is found not only in Hinduism and Buddhism, but also among the Sufis in Islam and the Hasidic movement in Judaism.

We come now to ask ourselves what is the future of contemplative life based on this tradition in the Church and the world. In the first place, I think that we must recognize that the Christian tradition cannot stand alone. We are being challenged today to see our religion in the context of other religions of the world. Since the way of meditation is found in all religions, contemplative life must be seen as a calling for humanity. We are moving out of a materialist civilization centred on science and technology into a new age in which people all over the world are consciously turning to a spiritual path, seeking to integrate their lives by bringing everything into the inner centre of the heart and finding the meaning of life, not in the external world, but in the inner reality of which the external world is a reflection. It is in the context of this new world that we have to see the place of contemplative life in the Church and the place of Christian communities in fostering this way of life.

I keep coming back to the view that the external world is a reflection, as in a mirror, of an interior world. In modern physics it is understood that beneath the outward appearances, first of external bodies, then of atoms, protons and electrons, there is a field of energies. We have to recognize that we ourselves are a field of energy functioning within the vast fields of energy of the universe. We project this three-dimensional world around us through our senses and our minds. That world is transitory. It is an expression of the vast mystery of energy in which we live and which we have to transcend. We are always mistaking outer phenomena, appearances, the world in space and time, for the reality, but we are slowly learning that all this is passing away. These are the great insights of India.

The Buddha, I think, had the most profound insight of any human being into the nature of the universe, because he saw through the world of appearances, of the senses. He saw it as all passing away. 'All is passing, all is sorrow.' There is no final satisfaction in this world. 'All is unreal', without substance, without any real base to it. We live in a world of passing phenomena; everything is changing all the time; all is in flux and conflict. But, as in a mirror or lake, the world reflects the divine reality under changing forms. At the moment of death, we pass beyond the flux of phenomena and the body as we know it, and enter into the reality. It is a little like watching a TV screen. We see the events going on and, if we didn't know better, we might think that they are happening there. But they are not happening on the screen. They are somewhere beyond what we are seeing, which is but a re-presentation. So the whole physical world is a re-presentation, a manifestation of an unseen reality.

Every religious tradition has a word for this unseen reality. In India we have *Brahman*. That is what is behind all phenomena, the

75

one everlasting *Brahman*. And behind the human body, there is *Atman*, the one self. The Buddha called it *nirvana* when all phenomena pass away. There is a 'blowing out' of all appearances, all change and becoming, and one enters the Eternal Reality. In the later Buddhist tradition, the reality is called *sunyata,* the void which is both fullness and emptiness.

In China there is the Tao. Confucius and his followers had their rituals and their strictly organized political and social life, but the great sage Lao Tsu saw behind all this to *Tao,* the way or river of the universe, which is behind everything yet cannot be seen. Lao Tsu used beautiful illustrations to explain the value of emptiness. 'We make spokes in a wheel in order to drive a chariot, but it is the empty space in the hub that enables the wheel to go around. We make pots of clay, but it is the empty space in the pot that makes it useful. We build houses of brick and mortar and wood, but it is the empty spaces in the doors and windows that make the house habitable.'

In the Muslim tradition, the Sufi Ibn Al Arabi showed that behind the God of the Koran is Al Haqq — the Reality. In Judaism, in the *Kabbala,* there are references to *ein sof,* the infinite. Behind Yahweh, the Law, the Prophets, and everything, is *ein sof*, the infinite. We are all discovering behind the projections of the physical world and even of religion, the reality that we are seeking. Karl Rahner called it 'the holy mystery', the mystery beyond everything. That is the goal of our religious search. We need a physical world and we need the symbols of religion, but we have to go beyond them to the reality.

We cannot do better than compare the present state of the world with that of the world in which Christianity was born. Jesus was born into a world in which there was an eager expectation of a new age. Jesus lived at the beginning of a new age that was not only promised by the Hebrew prophets but also mentioned by Virgil in his fourth Eclogue. In Israel, people were looking for the coming of the Messiah who would bring the present world to an end and inaugurate the Kingdom of God. It was in response to this that Jesus came preaching that 'the Kingdom of God is at hand'. Clearly he was conscious that he was inaugurating a new age. Many people expected the change to coincide with the destruction of the Roman Empire and the establishment of the political kingdom of a Messiah in Israel. Some have read the Book of Revelation in that spirit. But that was not Jesus' view. He saw that the new age could not be a continuation of the present world in space and time. He had to die to this world and everything in it. Only then could the new age begin. This is what took place at the resurrection. Jesus died to the world of appearances and inaugurated the new age of the resurrection.

The resurrection does not consist merely of the appearances of Jesus to his disciples after his death. Many think that these appearances in Galilee and Jerusalem are the resurrection. But they are simply to confirm the faith of the disciples. The real resurrection is the passing beyond the world altogether. It is Jesus' passage from this world to the Father. It was not an event in space and time, but the passage beyond space and time to the eternal, to reality. Jesus passed into the reality. That is our starting point.

It is into that world that we are invited to enter by contemplation. We do not have to wait for physical death, but can enter now into that eternal world. We have to go beyond the outer appearances of the senses and beyond the inner concepts of the mind, and open ourselves to the reality of Christ within, the Christ of the resurrection. Do not let us ever forget that the Christ within is the Christ of the resurrection. Just as the Christ of the Eucharist is the Christ of the resurrection. Some people do not quite realize that. He is really present in the resurrection. Jesus said, 'It is expedient for you that I go from you, for if I do not go, the Spirit will not come.' Jesus departs in the flesh to become present in the Spirit. In contemplation we encounter not Christ in the flesh, but Christ in the Spirit.

Christ is present to each one of us in the depths of the soul beyond the mind and the senses. The call of the Church today is to transcend the limits of the institutional structures and to open itself to the presence of the Spirit in the Church and in every Christian. All sacraments belong to the world of signs. A sacrament is a sign in which the reality is present. The bread and wine are signs, and the reality of Christ is present under those signs. All sacraments are manifestations of the presence of the divine reality under spatial-temporal signs.

The Church grew up in the Roman Empire and developed all its structures of sacrament, doctrine, and canon law based on the cultural inheritance of that civilization. But these structures are now growing obsolete. We have lived for almost 1900 years in these structures of the Greco-Roman world. In the first century of the New Testament, these structures were latent, but they had not yet emerged. It is only from the second century that sacraments, dogmas, priesthood and bishops, and all the structures of the Church emerged. We can say it was a movement of the Holy Spirit and that it has all grown out of the New Testament and the teachings of Jesus, but expressed in the terms of a particular historical culture. As long as we remain in this world, we need structures of doctrine and discipline to guide us on our way, but we have always to be looking beyond the structures, beyond the sacraments and doctrines to the Reality which they represent. Sacraments and doctrines represent, make present in human terms, the transcendent reality which cannot properly be expressed in human terms.

The Church is the 'sacrament of Christ', the sign of the real presence of Christ, as Christ is the sacrament of God. Christ is the sign of the real presence of God in humanity, the sign on earth of the eternal reality. God is present in the whole creation, in every-thing. He is present in you and me, but present under the signs of the sense phenomena of our bodies and souls. God is present in ritual and doctrine and law, but these are signs of a presence that transcends, and we have to go through signs always to the reality. Idolatry consists in worshipping signs. You stop with the sign. That is what an idol is. The Hebrew prophets were always denouncing the idols of the people. In India no true Hindu worships an image. They always know that the image is simply a sign of the divine presence. Hindus do not worship the image of wood or stone, but the divine presence within the wood or stone.

I had a nice experience once when we had a seminar on prayer at the National Centre in Bangalore. We invited a well-known Hindu pandit to attend. He was very friendly and had a great interest in Christianity, and he gave some excellent talks on the Hindu idea of sacrament. He celebrated a *puja* in his room and several of us attended. I had never been to a private *puja* before. He brought a little statue along with him and consecrated it. Once this was done, the God was really present in the statue. He worshipped and prayed, and then he deconsecrated the statue and put it back in his bag. It is very practical. But there is no doubt that the genuine Hindu always recognizes the presence under the sign. There was a great Hindu philosopher in the fourteenth century who said, 'God who is invisible in himself becomes visible in the image. God who is far away becomes nearer in the image. God who cannot be touched, can be touched in the image.' This is the Hindu understanding of sacrament.

Some signs are very imperfect, some are better. None is adequate to the reality. The whole world of nature is an imperfect manifestation of God. The call today is to transcend this world of signs and symbols, and enter the new creation, the new world which is revealed in all the great traditions. This is the call of humanity today. We are all involved in it. In the course of time, each religion developed its own structures of doctrine and ritual and law, but all have their cultural limitations. Christianity is originally a Semitic religion based on Hebrew scriptures translated into Greek and organised by Rome. It is a unique revelation of the divine within a definite historical and cultural context. We have to recognize the divine and, at the same time, be aware of the historical limits.

With Jesus and the resurrection a new age has dawned. The real world, which he called the Kingdom of God, was revealed. Humanity was called to enter the Kingdom, to pass beyond space and time, and to enter eternal reality. Jesus always spoke of the Kingdom in this way. He used parables to point to what cannot be put into words. He himself said, 'I have a baptism to undergo. How I am straitened until it is accomplished.' He had to go through death in order to enter into the new world, the world of communion with God. We have to go through death with him. It is the only way. This is the challenge that faces the world today. We are passing out of one world, the world of Western domination, and entering a new age in which the logical, rational mind of Greek philosophy and Roman law, the economic and political order, the science and technology of the West, will pass away. Our patriarchal culture is passing away at this present moment.

Something new is emerging. Nobody knows exactly what form it is going to take. It is a moment of trauma, of birth. We are waiting until all the present forms and structures pass away, and we shall see the whole universe in space and time and the whole of humanity redeemed by Christ standing in the fullness of reality. We are in this world of appearances, and we are waiting until the appearances pass and we see the reality behind them. That is the coming of the Kingdom of God. For Christ is that fullness of which it is said, 'In him all the fullness of the Godhead was pleased to dwell.' Again, it is said, 'The Church is the fullness of him who fills all in all.' Jesus is the fullness in which that divine reality becomes present in history and in time. The Church and we ourselves are part of that *pleroma,* that fullness, in which God is becoming present in humanity, in us.

It may seem a lot to suggest that the half hour of meditation, morning and evening, can open the mind to such a vision, but it was Father John's conviction that this is possible, and not just for monks and nuns but for everyone. We have to remember that the meditation with a mantra must always be sustained by faith and love, which alone can lead to contemplation. There is a danger if the mantra is treated as magic. The mantra is only a formula, and if you go on using it in faith it will lead to meditation and contemplation. But, like any form, it can become a psychological mechanism that leads nowhere. It must be sustained by faith. Faith is the opening of the inner heart, the inner spirit, to the reality of God. Faith is precisely that movement beyond to the transcendent mystery, and love is that movement of the heart through which we are united to that mystery. Faith and love take us beyond appearances to reality. This is the call of the Church and of humanity today. A new age is dawning, as it was in the time of Christ, and is so, in a sense, at all times. The new age is always coming. The Kingdom of God is always 'at hand', but usually in stages. Sometimes it comes at a critical moment, as it did in the time of Christ. I think it is coming today. This is a critical moment in human history.

The resurrection is a timeless event. It is a passage from the old into the new. Because Jesus passed from this world of space and time into the eternal reality, he is now wholly present in space and time. Once you get beyond the limited horizon of space and time, as he does in the resurrection, you become totally present to all space and time. God is present everywhere, in everything. Sometimes I illustrate it like this: In time there is a beginning, a middle and an end. And you go along that path. Eternity does not consist of going on and on and on like that. Eternity is always there and it is present equally at the beginning, the middle and the end. When you die, you do not simply go on to another life, but you pass beyond into the eternal reality which you *are* in your real being.

The new age is dawning, and it is a passage from the old into the new. As St Paul wrote in the letter to the Corinthians, 'If anyone is in Christ, there is a new creation. Everything old has passed away. Everything has become new.'[1] That happened in the time of the New Testament, and it is happening today. It is always happening. The old is always passing away and the new is always coming into birth. But we can be insensitive to this, by clinging to the old and thinking, 'This is it.' Then we stop the movement of creation.

Instead, we can allow things to grow and to move and enter into the new creation. That is what we are challenged to do.

The seer of the Apocalypse wrote, 'I saw a new heaven and a new earth. The first heaven and the first earth had passed away.'[2] That is, the temporal-spatial structure that we are building up will pass away. 'The one seated on the throne said, "Behold, I make all things new."'[3] That is the promise. The whole of this world is passing away, and the new creation is always there. It is reflecting itself in time. When time passes away, the eternal becomes manifest. The threat to the very existence of the earth has never been so severe. Many of you may have read *The Dream of the Earth* by Thomas Berry,[4] a Passionist Father from New York, who has given his life to the study of the earth and evolution. He points to the terrible tragedy that is being enacted on the planet through technology. We are ruining the earth with pollution of the air and water and the deterioration of the ozone layer which protects us from harmful rays of the sun. The great rain forests which are a source of life for the entire planet are rapidly being destroyed. They are being cut down, square miles at a time by big financial firms in Brazil and elsewhere. That which has taken billions of years to grow is being destroyed in a matter of decades. This is what is happening to our planet.

All these disasters are signs of rebirth. The disaster is coming, but a new creation is coming out of the disaster, from death to resurrection. The people of the earth today are all in trouble. Whole nations are changing their way of life. A system of government that threatened to dominate the world has suddenly dissolved. The situation in the former Soviet Union is one of the most dramatic in history. In the early days of the Russian Revolution, philosophers and theologians and others were saying that a new age had come and Marxism was the future of humanity. Many thought that the Soviet Union would eventually control the world, and at times it looked that way. Communism spread beyond Russia to China, and to parts of Africa and South America. A nuclear war seemed

82

inevitable, and then, suddenly, the whole thing disintegrated. We are living in a world of tremendous drama, tragedy, and hope.

The Church is also undergoing a crisis, greater perhaps than ever before. The Second Vatican Council was a major breakthrough. The Roman Curia had prepared various *schemata* in advance, which were intended as a basis for discussion. But, one after another, these documents were simply thrown out by the bishops as unfit even for discussion. A revolution took place in the Catholic Church, which had opened our hearts to a new vision of the Church, which we are still trying to live with. But that was only a beginning. A vast evolution has still to take place. I would say that in the next ten years, more basic changes will occur. We have to see the Holy Spirit working in the world, in the Church, in our lives, transforming us day by day. If we respond to it, then the new age will dawn.

It is only in the awakening of the contemplative spirit, of a transcendent consciousness, that we come to this vision of unity. The method of realizing this vision has been close at hand in the way of meditation taught by Father John Main. I really feel that he made a breakthrough that has opened the way for Christians to go beyond the world of the senses and of concepts to the divine mystery itself and to allow that mystery to penetrate our lives and transform them. It is a simple method, and yet it is so radical and fundamental that it really can change the world. This method of meditation, together with others, is spreading throughout the world. We must not isolate the Christian practice from others, because all are in search of the transcendent reality, whether they be Hindu, Buddhist, Muslim, Jewish or some other. All serious meditation is trying to go beyond the world of the senses and the mind, to open itself to the divine mystery. You cannot name it, you cannot express it, you can only point towards it. In meditation, something in you opens up and the divine discloses itself. You cannot force it. You have to let go and allow it to reveal itself.

I have defined contemplation as 'the experience of God in the Spirit'. Beyond the body and soul, is the spirit, the *pneuma*, the *Atman*, and that is the point of union with God. All human beings have a point in the depths of their being where they are open to God himself. That is where contemplation takes us, to that point of communion with God. That is the goal of the monk and of every person who follows the calling to be one with God. Our human nature is called to be one with God. There is no other way. It is not exclusive to Christians, because the grace of God is offered to all. Jesus died for all humanity. He is the new man, the new Adam, who reconciles humanity with God and opens up human nature itself to the divine.

The Church was originally a community of the Spirit. People who received the gift of the Spirit, of which contemplation is a type, dedicated their lives to prayer. It is said that the apostles appointed deacons to 'serve tables' but they gave themselves to 'the word of God and prayer'. Prayer comes first. Neither serving nor preaching is good if you are not praying. If you have not got Christ within, you cannot give him to others. You can put words and doctrines before people, but that is not preaching the gospel. It is only when you have the gospel and Christ within that you can communicate it to others. This is fundamental and central to our Christian faith. Contemplation is the prayer of union. It is union with God in the Spirit.

The monastic order is, I suggest, a prophetic order in the Church. In the early Church there were prophets together with apostles and other ministries in the Church. The prophets were people inspired by the Holy Spirit who went about visiting different churches without belonging to any one of them. They had the spiritual gift to go and awaken the spirit in others. We have rather lost that vocation now, though many religious orders provide it in their own way. Abishiktananda, one of the founders of our own ashram in India, said, 'To preach the gospel primarily is not to communicate a lot of words, it is to communicate the Holy Spirit.' Unless our words come from the Holy Spirit within, they are not words of life that communicate the gospel. Always we come back to contemplation, union with God at the heart of Christian life. Everything is in that. That is our responsibility.

The monastic order is this prophetic order in the Church. The gospel is primarily not a word to be preached but the Spirit to be communicated. In your meditation groups, you are not preaching, but you are sharing the gift of the Spirit, and that is how it should be. The word is necessary. We have to prepare ourselves to meditate. These are necessary means, but the end is the experience of God in the Spirit. From the ecumenical point of view, the hope for the future is not so much in the union of the churches on a doctrinal or sacramental level. I doubt that we will ever reach that. There are so many differences about sacraments and doctrines. But the point is to recognize the unity that already exists in the Spirit. Every baptized Christian receives the Holy Spirit, and in that gift we are all already one. We divide with our rituals and doctrine, but the Holy Spirit is given to every Christian and, we must add, is given to every human being. All are created in the image of God, and that signifies the presence of the Spirit. At the point of the Spirit, we are already one. The ecumenical movement demands that we recognize this communion in the Spirit which we already share and which can grow.

St Paul says, 'No one can say, "Jesus is the Lord," except in the Holy Spirit.'[5] We cannot say that Jesus is Lord in a genuine way except in the Spirit. That is what we all share. Perhaps this gives us an ecumenical view of the future and our place in it. It is very important that God has brought us together and taught us meditation and shown us how to be the Church in a new way. Contemplative prayer is, I feel, the great need of the Church and the world today.

1 2 Corinthians 5:17.
2 Revelations 21:1.
3 Revelations 21:5.

4 Thomas Berry, *The Dream of the Earth*, Sierra 1990.
5 2 Corinthians 5:6.

6

Questions and Responses

Questions to Bede Griffiths at the seminar led him to express his thoughts on some further aspects of the subjects he had spoken about. The questions centred mostly on the way of meditation, on how meditation leads those who practise it into community with each other and to greater concern for others, and on aspects of Christian faith and life.

The Way of Meditation

QUESTION: Can we say that meditation will always lead to an experience of God's presence?
RESPONSE: I think that for most people the mantra is the way to open themselves to the inner life of the Spirit. Normally the mantra goes on continually and, as Father John always said, you let the mantra go on as long as it can. The purpose of the mantra is to go beyond the ego. But, once you let the mantra go, it is so easy for your ego to come in and the spiritual ego is the greatest danger of all. When you think you are getting very near to God, you are in fact getting more and more egotistical. I remember one Hindu *sannyasi* saying of another, 'He is ego from top to toe'!

Our belief is that the mantra keeps you humble. Father John always insisted that this is a very simple, humble way. 'Quietly repeating your word,' he says, keeps the ego in its place and should lead you to the transcendent. But, unless the mantra is accompanied by faith and love, it has no real value; it would be merely a mechanism. It is a real danger merely to trust the mechanism of the mantra, but as an expression of faith and love it becomes a very powerful means to direct your faith and love and to open you to God.

QUESTION: Are there guidelines for people trying to live a contemplative life in the world?

RESPONSE: This is a need we have to work on. We have to remember that a monk is not a priest, and it is very important to keep the two vocations completely distinct. In the early Church priests were nearly always married. In his Letter to Timothy Paul says that bishops should have only one wife,[1] so there was never then a question of whether he should have a wife or not. St Gregory of Nyssa, the greatest mystic among the Fathers, was married and was, I think, the son of a married priest. The problem began when, in the fourth century, monks began to be seen as the model of a Christian. St Anthony in particular became the model Christian, and priests and others began to model themselves on the monks. So the two vocations gradually blended and we have yet to get free of this. I became a priest simply because it was part of the process of my monastic vocation; we just went from profession to ordination. I did not make any specific choice and I hardly ever administered the sacraments.

I feel we have come to a point today where we must keep the two vocations separate and distinct. The monk is a lay person. St Benedict was not a priest, and the early Benedictine communities were 'lay communities'. The monk has his own unique vocation of prayer, of meditation and the surrender of his life to God. The priest on the other hand has a sacramental ministry. The monk should not normally be involved in a sacramental ministry, I think. A Hindu monk has a kind of funeral rite when he becomes a *sannyasi*. He dies to the social order and is not supposed to celebrate the *puja* again. The *puja* is the normal ritual carried out by a priest in the Hindu tradition. The *sannyasi* has gone beyond the social and sacramental dimension and belongs to God alone.

An order of monastics is essentially a lay order. Some monks may live in monasteries, but increasingly the majority will live in their own homes or form small communities — a monastic order in the world. That is rather like the Sufis, who are not priests. Often the Sufi is married, and the community gathers around the family. These are models we could easily follow, and this is perhaps the direction in which we are moving today.

QUESTION: What about the difficulty of teaching meditation to people who are not adequately aware of their own personhood?

RESPONSE: We need to remind ourselves that meditation is not only for Christians or those who believe in God, but also for many others who are really searching for deeper meaning in their lives. The point is, can they be led to see that the deeper meaning will come simply from sitting still for a time, and from a more disciplined life? They can be led into this, but it is difficult. Probably some people cannot do very much, and there are some social groups where people are so alienated that it is almost impossible to get this message across. We have simply to work within our limits. This is why I am always in favour of a group or community forming a centre to which people can be attracted. If instead you go out and encounter people in their own situation where they have no sense of God or their own meaning, I think it can be very difficult.

QUESTION: As Christian meditators how can we be totally Christian and yet completely open to other traditions?

RESPONSE: This is a difficult question. If we are too affirming of our Christian faith people will simply keep away from us. Many people in America have a very strong prejudice against Christianity; they know it from evangelists on TV and they hate it. In India also many Hindus hate Christianity. They will say they love Christ but do not like the way Christians behave in pressing their religion on people. On the other hand, it is no good being too ecumenical or we become syncretists. We have to learn how to have a clear commitment and a firm, clear faith, while at the same time being truly open to other ways of faith and commitment.

I think we are learning that through the ecumenical movement in the Christian churches. We are no longer trying to convert each other and have come to realize that we are standing for the same truth though within different traditions. We need also to be open to people of no religion, who yet are really sincere people searching for God. Evangelism today needs to be expressed in terms of mission and dialogue. It is no good simply putting your view to someone and expecting them to adopt it. You have to listen to them if they are to listen to you.

When I first came to India we started a little community outside Bangalore. There were four of us, and young Hindu students came up from the village out of curiosity. When they found that we were using the Upanishads and the Gita and knew far more about these scriptures than they did, they were very attracted. Some said, 'We have never known a Christian institution like this before.' Then, spontaneously, one after another, they began to ask about the life of Christ. If you show that you are open to others and understand them, then they begin to be open to you. But if you put your view first, it will often close doors. This is the secret, I think, both for India and the West.

Meditation and Community

QUESTION: What is a lay community and can a meditation group be one?

RESPONSE: There are various levels of *lay* community and several stages in its formation. I think the most important thing is that it should really be a lay community, and not become semi-clerical. The lay person has a definite status in the Church, while the religious or cleric has a different one. The local bishop should know of the community but that does not mean he should have responsibility for it. A lay community should be of lay people living and expressing their Christian life, ready to be guided by others but not under their authority. We need that freedom in the Church, responsible freedom. We should also be able to criticise the Church responsibly, because we love the Church and not because we are trying to cause trouble.

The first stage of a lay community is to meet together to meditate regularly. After some time, when a bond has grown up between you, you can say you form a kind of lay community, but only in a very general sense. The next stage, which many are moving into now, is when you definitely commit yourself as a community to share together, probably but not necessarily living together. Each group has to find its own style of association. Then, when you feel your little group is sharing a common life, then you begin to be a 'lay community'. You have then to let it grow, because it is the Holy Spirit that forms community.

In the Acts of the Apostles there is one of the great models for Christian community. We read that, after Pentecost, they met together, remaining "in the apostles' teaching, the *koinonia* [the community], the breaking of bread and the prayers".[2] In this you see the model of Christian community. Once there is the *koinonia,* the common life in Christ, there is the beginning of community, and then you let it grow. Some communities may remain very loose, some may become very close. Each one has to evolve as the Spirit moves it.

QUESTION: How can we give the worldwide community of Christian meditation a right kind of authority without becoming institutionalized?

RESPONSE: It is right that we must avoid the temptation to institutionalization. It seems much safer to have rules, but we are trying to get beyond that. Our meditation must lead us to a very real dependence on the Holy Spirit, and we must believe that the Holy Spirit is with us and is guiding us. Members of the early Church were very conscious of the Spirit guiding their every movement. St Paul once said he wanted to go somewhere 'but the Holy Spirit would not allow it'. Studies today in the early Church are revealing how very charismatic the first Christian churches were. They were communities of the Spirit, and it was only gradually that organization and institutionalization came in. This is almost inevitable as things grow. But we must keep that freedom of the Spirit by learning from one another, coming together day by day and discerning what God wants, all in a growth process. It is a real responsibility, and I think you must feel that in coming together in meditation you are being bonded together and that God is guiding you. That is all we can pray for.

QUESTION: If meditation leads us toward community, do we as lay people in community need to find a new language, to modify words like 'rules' and 'discipline'?

RESPONSE: It is a real challenge to find a new way to express our Christian life. It is so easy to get into rules and organization and so to narrow the freedom of the Spirit. The essential thing that Jesus left the Church was the Spirit. It is by learning really to trust the Spirit, in our prayer and meditation, and to share this trust with one another that a new language will gradually form. We need a Rule and some kind of organization, some proper discipline, if we are to avoid breaking apart. But this needs discernment day by day.

QUESTION: Can a lay community and a religious community be associated in such a way as to be mutually upbuilding and complementary?

RESPONSE: This is an important question. Until recently an oblate was just attached to a monastery, but this is not a very satisfactory relationship, in that it makes someone who visits a monastery and is attracted to a monastic style of life try to live in this spirit at home, but often in a dependent way. Now instead, we are thinking of lay communities which are much more independent. They may consult with a monastery and be open to guidance to develop their own style of life, particularly from a monk who is truly understanding of their need for independence, but they should not be dependent. Our prior at New Camaldoli, who is interested in lay communities, believes the monastery should not be responsible for them. Otherwise the monastery feels it has to interfere, and the lay community feels it must always have the approval of the monastery.

QUESTION: The ego destroys community. How can we build community?

RESPONSE: As soon as we form a community the ego in each person begins to come out. Of course, it is the same thing when one marries. It is the main problem of life. We each have a strong ego, and it is a good thing for our personality if we do. But it is always in conflict. The closer we come to people the more we are in conflict.

I remember a story of five soldiers stationed together in a very remote place. They became so exasperated living together that they set up a drum and they would go and beat this drum as hard as they could to get rid of their anger and frustration.

Through meditation we recognize the ego in ourselves, including our spiritual ego. We see how it upsets us and others, and gradually we overcome it and come to deeper love. We have to go through the conflict in order to come to this deeper relationship. That is how love is found. In the lay communities we are talking about, this surely will be the main problem. You come together to pray, to meditate, to share together, and then the different egos begin to come up and everything can easily disintegrate. It is a tremendous grace if you can forgive one another. 'Bearing with one another in love' is St Paul's phrase.[3]

I heard of a woman who had been in a concentration camp in Poland. Years later she met one of the Nazi officers who had become a Catholic. He came up to greet her and held out his hand. Her anger and resentment for what he had done to her was so great she could not take it. But then she prayed, simply entrusting her life to God, and she managed to forgive him. Perhaps we can never forgive as long as we think we are all in the right, but when we realize our own need for forgiveness we become capable of forgiving others.

So, in a community we have to get free of the ego by recognizing it in ourselves and in others and then learn to surrender it to God and allow the grace of God, the Holy Spirit, to take us beyond the ego. It is only beyond the ego that peace and reconciliation and love can find a place.

QUESTION: What is the importance of social action in relation to meditation?

RESPONSE: This question came to us in the ashram movement in India. There we were, living in ashrams, and what were we doing for the great multitudes of the poor? There have been different responses.

Some Catholic ashrams are much involved in social action and were founded mainly for that purpose. But our feeling is that the ashram is a centre where deeper awareness can grow. Then out of our meditation we should naturally become more aware of the problems of humanity and of our neighbourhood. Social action should flow from our contemplation. It should not be a sideline or something inherently different, but should be integrated in our prayer and meditation.

Personally, I have always found that unless meditation is fed by concern with people's problems and the world's problems it loses its depth. There is no rivalry between contemplation and action. There is a danger when people feel that because the world's problems are so demanding they must give their whole life to the poor in action. I remember a friend who joined a team working with the poor in Brazil. Their idea was that there was no need for Mass or prayer because Christ was in the poor. One had only to go out to the poor and one would meet Christ in them. So they gave up Mass and prayer and concentrated only on active service to the poor. Within a few years the work totally disintegrated. I think unless we find Christ within, we will not find him among the poor, though we may be doing good to them in various ways. The two are reciprocal: the more we find Christ within, the more we become aware of Christ without. There is a polarity here, one acting on the other.

QUESTION: Can you comment on the Father image of God?

RESPONSE: The Father-God is a serious problem for many people, especially for those who have a psychological history with their own father to work through. Some people of course have had a wonderful relationship with their father. It is important to introduce the image of God as mother. The one thing Pope John Paul I left to the Church was the saying, 'God is mother.' In India the mother image has always been stronger than the father image. Indians use both and will quite spontaneously speak of God as 'my mother, my father'. So strong is their sense of the motherhood of God that if you want to find the Catholic church in an Indian village you ask for the *'matha kovil'*, the mother-church where our Lady is. Our Lady has a tremendous power and for most Catholics it is the only archetype of the feminine. But this motherhood should be in our idea of God. God is no less mother than father, and so we are trying to develop a theology in which we can see the Holy Spirit as mother.

In Hebrew, the word *ruah*, spirit, is feminine. There is some significance in that, I think. In the Wisdom books, *hochmah* (the wisdom of God) is always feminine too. In the Book of Proverbs 'she' played before God at the creation of the world. The feminine quality of wisdom in the Wisdom of Solomon also shows that there are feminine images of God. Originally even the 'word' of God was feminine, as in Sanskrit. So we have to get used to thinking of God as both masculine and feminine; the one is needed to balance the other. It is urgent for most people to move beyond the exclusively masculine image, and this is an important part of theological development today.

QUESTION: What do you mean when you say that God is 'interpersonal communion'?

RESPONSE: Seeing God as a person is a very important stage. This is seen in the Old Testament and the Koran, and many of us address prayer to God in that way. But, strictly speaking, in the Christian tradition of the New Testament God is not a person; he is Father, Son and Holy Spirit. It all stems from the experience of Jesus, and Jesus did not experience himself as God. We have got into the habit of talking of Jesus as God, and this is theologically correct, but it is not the way he experienced himself. He never speaks of himself as God. It would actually have been absurd to do so.

To Jesus the Father was God and his whole life was directed towards his Father and their communion. Later his disciples realized that this communion was of two in one, and the idea of the Trinity gradually evolved. Jesus shared his communion with the Father with his disciples in the Holy Spirit; as St John's gospel describes it — 'that they may be one as you in me and I in you, that they may be one is us'.[4] The unity we have with Jesus and the Father is the unity of the Holy Spirit. Each of us enters into communion with Jesus in the Father through the Holy Spirit. Trinity is the essence, the very ground of all Christian existence. It is not one person. It is the communion of love. The traditional way to express this is that God is found in relationship.

The whole life of Father Mochanin (the founder of our ashram) centred on the Trinity. When he died in Paris of cancer in 1957 he was meditating and discoursing on the Trinity on his deathbed. He was a great theologian who always said that *esse* (in Latin, to be) is always *'coesse'* (to 'be with'); to be is to be in relationship. There is no such thing as being that is not in relationship. So the Being of Reality expresses itself in relationship, and the expression of this relationship is the Word of God. And then it communicates itself in love in the Spirit, and the Spirit is the communication of being in love.

Unfortunately the Greeks turned the Trinity into an abstract theological dogma which is totally unreal to most people. The reality is that Jesus communicates the Holy Spirit to us and in the Holy Spirit he invites us to be one with the Father. It is part of our inner life We are in the Holy Trinity. It is in us and it is our life.

QUESTION: Who is the Cosmic Christ?

RESPONSE: I think it is helpful to speak of the cosmic revelation. There are two stages of revelation. It began before Christ in a cosmic religion. For example, the Australian aborigines have had a deep religion for 40,000 years. Other ancient peoples, like the native Americans and the African tribal peoples, have a sense of the sacred presence in nature, in the earth, sun and moon, stars, plants and animals as well as in humans. They live in a sacred universe. This form of religion could be badly abused and lead to superstition and false doctrines, but it has a real core of truth. God is seen to be in the earth and in the whole creation. The cosmic Christ, then, is our belief that Christ himself goes beyond space and time, is totally one with the Father, the creator-God, and so is also present in all creation.

St Paul says, 'He who descended is also he who ascended that he might fill all things,[5] and 'In him and through him and for him all things are created and in him all things hold together.'[6] The whole universe holds together in Christ: that is the cosmic Christ. It needs to be said that Christ is present in all religion. Jesus died for all humanity, without exception. So, from the beginning to the end of the world the grace of Christ through the cross is offered to every human being in some way, normally through their conscience, their traditions and customs or holy books. The Second Vatican Council said that the 'Church rejects nothing that is true and holy in other religions'. There is truth and holiness in all genuine religion. Their knowledge and understanding is often very imperfect, but it can grow. The Christian mission is to help other people to grow but also to learn from them so that our Christian faith grows too. It has been our experience in the ashram that the more we open ourselves to the other religions, to Hinduism in particular, the deeper our Christian faith grows. Our aim is the deepening of our own faith which then becomes more open to others.

This is not easy, and everybody has to answer the question for themselves. I like the illustration of fingers and the palm of the hand. The fingers represent Buddhism, Hinduism, Islam, Judaism and Christianity. Buddhism is miles from Christianity, and each has its own position. If you try to mix them, taking a bit of Hinduism or Buddhism and adding it to Christianity, that is syncretism. But if you go deeply into any one tradition you converge on a centre, and there you see how we all come forth from a common root. And you find how we meet people on the deeper level of their faith in the profound unity behind all our differences.

Father Monchanin and Father le Saux, the founders of our ashram, were holy men in this regard. Father Monchanin in particular saw how we had to meet the Hindus at the source of their religion in the Upanishads, the Vedas, the Gita. In Christianity the source is in the New Testament, the early Fathers and first monks. But if you look to the seventeenth or eighteenth century, with all their complications, it is very difficult to meet. It is in the source we discover unity. Our spiritual journey today is to go back to the source of all religions. Christ is ultimately the source of all religion. He is behind it all.

QUESTION: Even if a person does not believe in spiritual forces — such as demons and angels — as a reality, do they affect that person?

RESPONSE: To most people angels and demons have lost all reality and are just like elves and fairies — fantasies. I think there is a psychological explanation of them as autonomous entities in the unconscious. They work in us and in humanity as a whole. They are cosmic forces, destructive and creative. This is the meaning of the Christian doctrine of the fall of the angels. The angels are spiritual powers, presences that come from God. An angel is a mode of the divine presence. In the Old Testament there is hardly any distinction between the angels and God, as we see in the story of the three who came and dined with Abraham.

An angel can turn away from God, the source of its being, and centre on itself. A self-centred spiritual power like this becomes a demonic, destructive power, and these can act in and through the human unconscious. Hitler is a perfect example. He undoubtedly had occult power and was touched by occult forces, which he allowed to work in him and build up a tremendous power of violence and destruction.

There is an extraordinary book called *Meditations on the Tarot.*[7] It is by a Russian who wrote it anonymously before his death in, I think, 1967. He was a Lutheran to begin with, entered Anthroposophy and then became a very devout Catholic. He interprets all these phenomena, with great insight into angels and demons in the context of Christian faith. He had a profound intuition of the psychic and spiritual world and his book helped to convince me that we must treat these as real forces today. All the tragedies taking place in South Africa or Palestine are not simply of human origin. As St Paul says, our conflict is not with flesh and blood but with spiritual powers in the high places. Demonic forces are at work, and I think we have to take them seriously, because they are in all of us.

QUESTION: Can you speak about the relations between the fall of Man and the body?

RESPONSE: The human being is created body, soul and spirit. St Irenaeus, in the second century, had the great idea that the first man was not, as St Thomas Aquinas thought, a perfect man of supreme intelligence, but a 'child man'. He had to grow but he was innocent. His body and soul were created to respond to the Spirit. God was speaking to him in the Spirit and, if he had not fallen, he would have grown in body and soul to an ever deeper relationship with God and with others. The whole creation would have been as it was intended. But instead of responding to the spirit within he centred on the ego, on himself. Once that happens you fall into your ego, a separated self, separated from God, from others and from the universe around you.

We are all centred in this ego, and meditation and all Christian practice is a way of going beyond the ego and opening up to the Spirit and then allowing the Spirit to transform us. We cannot transform ourselves. But the moment we go beyond the ego, beyond its rational consciousness, we enter the non-dual consciousness where we see everybody and everything as distinct but not separate. Fritjof Capra, in his *Tao of Physics*[8] talks of the universe as a 'complicated web of interdependent relationships'. Everything in this universe is interdependent and interrelated.

QUESTION: As Christians we can be redeemed by Christ's love. How do people of other faiths get redeemed without Christ?

RESPONSES: What we understand today, and what was understood traditionally, is that Jesus died for all humanity, not just for the Jews or Christians. He is called the 'Second Adam'. Adam is humanity which falls away from God and is involved in sin, suffering and death. Jesus is the new Adam who reconciles humanity with God. One of the early Church councils said there is no human being whose nature is not redeemed by Christ. We are all born into a common human nature which is both fallen and redeemed. The grace of Christ is present in some way to every human being from the beginning to the end. Normally it comes through their traditional religion.

This is why we have a sense today of Christ present in all religions, from that of the most primitive Australian aborigines on. Its mode of expression, of course, may be very limited but it is a real presence. Anybody who corresponds to grace and truth in their lives is present to Christ. The Second Vatican Council made it clear in the Constitution on the Church that everyone — Catholics, all Christians, Jews, Muslims, all who believe in God, and even those who do not but seek to follow their conscience — is open to salvation.

We would say then that Jesus Christ is present to every human being, offering this grace of truth and love. An atheist is often a person who has rejected a bad image or concept of God. Yet he may

100

feel strongly that he is following the truth. We would say he is following Christ. So, when we come to the last judgement, people will discover that behind all the forms and images which they worshipped is the real presence of the love of Christ. That to me is a certain fact.

In India the Christian used to look at the Hindu and see a pagan under the power of the devil from which he must be rescued. But now we try to see that Christ is already present. Our call is to draw out that presence of Christ, to make them realize it more and more fully. In India sometimes you meet the most Christlike people among Hindus, and there is no doubt that the Presence is there.

QUESTION: What does discernment actually mean in terms of deciding whether something is really 'of the spirit' or not?

RESPONSE: Discernment of spirits is a very ancient tradition which the Fathers spoke about frequently. I think we just have to learn it by experience — and make big mistakes. Sometimes you think God is saying something but it turns out to be illusion, because the Spirit always works with the psyche and the psyche has the ego in it. So if we are not careful the ego corrupts the spiritual. It is only watchfulness that helps. Through meditation we remain watchful all the time to see if the ego is getting into our thoughts, our feelings, our actions. Our behavior gives us away a great deal.

People ask, 'How can I know the will of God'? It is very difficult. You can only know it by experience, by trying, by making mistakes. In time you find you are getting guidance. This is one of the most important effects of meditation, that you begin to find a guidance in your life: that you are guided to meet the right people, to go to the right place, to do the right thing, and you begin to see that you are not managing your life just by yourself. God himself is acting in you. It is a very specific grace of meditation when you get that sense of guidance in your life, a visible sign; it is akin to what Jung called synchronicity.

A Japanese doctor once gave me a book she had written on the Tao of psychology. (Tao is the Chinese term for the 'order of the universe'.) She had read a lot on Jung's concept of synchronicity and related it to the Tao as the rhythm of the universe. We are part of this rhythm, and once we tune into it things begin to happen. We do not have to plan everything ahead. If we are attentive and watchful and flow with the rhythm, then we do the right thing and we are moved by the Spirit. The Tao is the Spirit of God working through the whole world. It is the guidance we get in our life day by day.

QUESTION: Suffering in the world seems inevitable. How do you account for the suffering of innocent people, of children for example, relative to a God who is love?

RESPONSE: I try to see this question in the context of body, soul and spirit. We tend to see suffering in terms of the body. People are killed or they suffer from cancer in hospital, and it all seems very tragic. But even in a state of great physical suffering there can be an inner peace and joy. I remember a story of somebody who was almost completely paralysed, whose reply to someone's consoling remarks was, 'I am as happy as can be.' Joy is not contrary to suffering as pleasure is. We need to see further than the physical side of suffering. Television can do a lot of harm by showing only the outer side of suffering.

Suffering of the soul, psychological suffering, is the next level and is much more serious. Yet even here we can overestimate its importance, as we see when we have passed through a traumatic time and realize that it was transient. The third level, of spirit, is where suffering can become creative and transforming. Once you learn to get beyond your physical suffering and psychological feelings and be open to the point of the spirit, then suffering becomes not only tolerable but transforming.

When Jesus was dying on the cross there was his body, humiliated and bleeding, looking horrible. He was also suffering in the soul. He felt deeply in himself the rejection by his people. But behind all that Jesus in the depth of his spirit was always in communion with the Father. At this deep level there is total transcendence.

People working in the hospice movement often encounter the stages of suffering in their patients: anger and resentment, leading to depression. But once they learn really to accept their suffering and open themselves to God, an extraordinary tranquility comes and they can see the suffering as a blessing. I am more and more convinced that when any of these tragedies occurs, it is then that the greatest grace comes.

I will tell of you my experience when I had a stroke. It was in January 1990. I was meditating at six o'clock one morning and something came and hit me on the head. It felt like a sledge-hammer. Everything went blurred, like a television screen before it is focused. A terrible force was pushing me out of my chair and I did not know what was happening. I managed to crawl on to the bed and I was found there after about an hour. Apparently I was unconscious for a week. No, I was conscious, but I did not speak and I have no memory of it at all. But there were some wonderful people in the ashram and they arranged everything for me each day. At the end of a week I began to come round to normal consciousness and there was a profound change. It was really that I had died to the ego, I think. The ego-mind, and also maybe the discriminative mind that separates and divides, all seemed to have gone. Everything was flowing into everything else, and I had a sense of unity behind it all. Then this began to open up. I thought I was going to die and I really prepared for it. That was very important. We all ought to be ready to die tonight. We have to let go of everything, because our lives are in the hands of God. We should be ready to let go of the soul and body into the hands of God. I sort of let go, and nothing in particular happened.

Then somebody came and massaged me and I came back to normal. A very important experience then happened. I felt rather restless and uncertain and an urge came to me to 'surrender to the mother'. I made this surrender and an overwhelming experience of love came over me. It was like waves of love. I called out to someone who was watching there, 'I am being overwhelmed by love!'

I think what happened was a psychological breakthrough to the feminine. In each person there is both masculine and feminine, and most men repress the feminine. I have done that to a very considerable extent, and I think it was the woman in me who came and hit me on the head! But then she came back to me as a loving mother. When you let the feminine open and your unconscious lets her come up, then she is the loving mother and in coming back to you she transforms you. Because God is mother we have to balance the masculine and the feminine in our nature. We must be aware of how we are repressing one aspect of our nature; by allowing it to come up we become whole.

That stroke was a wonderful experience and the greatest grace I have ever had in my life. You don't need to have a stroke, but don't be upset if you do. Or if you get cancer or AIDS. These can be a grace of God, a moment when your transformation takes place and your whole ego, your whole life, dissolves. Something new then comes. I think we all have to go through this. Many of you have gone through traumatic experiences — a divorce, the loss of your husband or wife, or child. These things may seem a disaster, but they are precisely the moment when a new birth can take place and a new understanding of life and yourself follows.

So, when you see people being killed, suffering in hospital and so on, remember this is on the physical level, and the psychological level. But the hidden mystery behind all the pain and suffering and disaster of the world is a tremendous ocean of love. And I am sure that when we die we shall discover this ocean of love which is hidden from us now.

Behind all the conflict and confusion is this hidden mystery of love that is behind the whole universe. It is hidden, but tragedies enable us to become awake to it. I think that will be the great awakening in death for everybody. For many, death is going through the darkness of destruction. That is how I see Jesus on the cross. He lost everything. He was rejected by his people, persecuted by the Romans; all his disciples had left him and fled. He was there alone, in pain and humiliation, having lost everything. 'My God, my God, why have you forsaken me?' I think he felt forsaken by God: God is always a projection of some sort and we always have some image. The Father whom he trusted all his life seemed to have left him. At that very moment of total death, total surrender and letting everything go, he was transformed into total love. He revealed the total love which goes beyond death.

Today we are going through a time of disintegration, what in India they call *Kali yuga*. Everything is breaking up, politically, socially, economically, religiously. But, at the same time as we think we are disintegrating in death, there is a new birth, a new creation coming into being. People discover this new dimension in their lives very often through tragedy.

Encounter of East and West

QUESTION: What do the East and West have to teach each other? RESPONSE: In the West our religion is extravert. We tend to go out, to God, to Christ, to people. The Church in India is renowned for its charity. A Dominican priest was once talking to his friend, a Hindu professor, in north India. He asked the Hindu, 'What do you think of us Christians?' The Hindu hesitated and then replied, 'I think you are very good people and I admire all your good works, but I cannot see that you have any *religion*.' By 'religion' he meant, for example, a *suddhu* living a simple, austere life of meditation in solitude. Christians generally stand for charitable organization rather than the interior life. What we have to learn from the Buddhists and the Hindus is their interiority.

Some people used to talk about the 'forgotten Paraclete'. We had the Father in heaven and we had Jesus, but the Paraclete was forgotten. The Paraclete is the 'spirit within'. This is what God is teaching us today through meditation. We are beginning to discover this inner life and we have learned it from the mantra.

Of course, learning from each other carries the danger of syncretism. Most Hindus I know are syncretists; they think it is all the same whether you believe in Jesus, Krishna, Rama or Buddha. We are not syncretists like that, but we do believe that each religion has its own unique value and insights which we need to share with one another. We have our own unique way through revelation in Christ and through the Church. We try to share that with others, but we recognize too that God has revealed himself in other ways to other people, and so we try to recognize their values. Respect for other people's religion and culture is the crucial thing and I think, on the whole, this is the way the Church is moving today.

1 1 Timothy 3:2.
2 Acts 2:42.
3 Ephesians 4:2.
4 John 17:21.
5 Ephesians 4:10.
6 Colossians 1:16.
7 *Meditations on the Tarot,* new edn, Element Books 1991.
8 Fritjof Capra, *Tao of Physics*, Fontana 1976.

Writings of Bede Griffiths

The Golden String (Templegate, 1954 and 1980)
Christ in India (Templegate, 1966/1984)
Vedanta and Christian Faith (Dawn Horse Press, 1973)
Return to the Center (Templegate, 1978)
The Marriage of East and West (Templegate, 1983)
The Cosmic Revelation (Templegate, 1987)
River of Compassion: A Christian Commentary on the Bhagavad-gita (Amity House, 1988)
Christianity in the Light of the East (Hibbert Trust, 1989)
A New Vision of Reality (Templegate, 1990)
Bede Griffiths (Modern Spirituality Series: Templegate, 1992)
The New Creation in Christ (Templegate, 1994)

The recorded texts of Bede Griffiths at the John Main Seminar of 1991 are available as a boxed set of six cassettes, *Christian Meditation: The Evolving Tradition,* from Medio Media Ltd, 23 Kensington Square, London W8 5HN (£25 plus p&p).

Writings of John Main

Word into Silence (London, Darton, Longman and Todd, 1980; New York, Paulist Press, 1981)

Letters from the Heart (New York, Crossroad, 1982)

Moment of Christ (London, DLT, 1984; New York, Crossroad, 1984)

The Present Christ (London, DLT, 1985; New York, Crossroad, 1985)

The Inner Christ (London, DLT, 1987). Combines *Word into Silence, Moment of Christ, the Present Christ*

The Joy of Being: Daily Readings with John Main (London, DLT, 1987)

The Heart of Creation (London, DLT, 1988; New York, Crossroad, 1988)

The Way of Unknowing (London, DLT, 1989; Crossroad, 1989)

John Main (Modern Spirituality Series: Templegate, 1989)

There are two biographical studies of John Main:

Neil McKenty, *In the Stillness Dancing* (London, Darton, Longman and Todd, 1986; New York, Crossroad, 1987)

Paul Harris (ed.), *John Main by those Who Knew Him* (London, Darton, Longman and Todd, 1991; Ottawa, Novalis, 1991)

The World Community for Christian Meditation

It was John Main's belief that the contemplative experience creates community. His genius was to recover and re-present a way into this experience for ordinary people from within the Christian contemplative tradition. In the teaching of the Desert Monks he found the practice of the mantra or pure prayer. Realizing that this way of prayer answered the needs of modern people for a deeper spiritual life he recommended two regular daily periods of meditation to be integrated with the usual practice of Christian life.

It has become increasingly evident in recent years that meditation as a way of tolerance and compassion forms a bridge of the Spirit between peoples of different faith, between rich and poor, and between all those in opposition or misunderstanding. The great social, spiritual and psychological distresses of modern society call for a deep contemplative response. John Main believed strongly in the contemplative life as a call to each human being whatever their position or lifestyle. It is an expression of this that his teaching is most commonly passed on through weekly meditation groups run by lay people.

The World Community for Christian Meditation was called into being and formed into a flexible structure by the participants at the John Main Seminar led by Bede Griffiths in New Harmony, Indiana in 1991. Its avowed aim is to encourage and nurture the practice of meditation in the Christian tradition as taught by John Main in the spirit of serving the unity of all. Meditation groups following this teaching meet in over thirty-five countries, in homes, parishes, colleges, prisons and communities. A number of Christian Meditation Centres (see below) participate in this Community each in their unique way. The coherence of the Community is found in the teaching of John Main and a wide variety of expressions are being integrated. The link with the monastic tradition, particularly the Benedictine, is highly valued and new forms of community life are encouraged.

The International Centre:

23 Kensington Square
London W8 5HN
Tel and fax: 071 937 4679

Christian Meditation Centres:

Australia
Christian Meditation Network
10 Grosvenor Road
Glen Iris VIC 3146
Tel: 03 822 4870

Belgium
Christelijk Meditatie Centrum
Beiaardlaan 1
1850 Grimbergen
Tel: 02 269 5071

Canada
Christian Meditation
   Community
PO Box 552 Station NDG
Montreal, Quebec H4A 3P9
Tel: 514 766 0475

India
Christian Meditation Centre
1/1429 Bilathikulam Road
Calicut
Kerala 673006
Tel: 495 60395

Ireland
Christian Meditation Centre
62 Park Avenue
Dublin 4
Tel: 1 693 466

New Zealand
Christian Meditation Centre
PO Box 139
Orewa
Tel: 0942 63 891

Philippines
Christian Meditation Centre
L4B Champaca Road, UPS IV
1700 Paranaque
Metro Manila
Tel: 03 827 63

Singapore
Christian Meditation Centre
Holy Family Church
6 Chapel Road
Singapore 1542
Tel: 344 0046

Thailand
Christian Meditation Groups
51/1 Sedsiri Road
Bangkok 10400
Tel: 271 3295

United Kingdom
Christian Meditation Centre
29 Campden Hill Road
London W8 7DX
Tel: 071 937 0014

United States of America
John Main Institute
7315 Brookville Road
Chevy Chase MD 20815
Tel: 301 652 8635

Christian Meditation Centre
1080 West Irving Park Road
Roselle IL 60172
Tel: 708 351 2613

Christian Meditation Centre
Church of the Transfiguration
1 East 29th Street
New York, NY 10016
Tel: 212 684 6770

Hesed Community
3745 Elston Avenue
Oakland CA 94602
Tel: 415 482 5573